Developmental Psychology

Volume V

Student Handbook to Psychology

Developmental Psychology

Volume V

LYNN M. SHELLEY

Bernard C. Beins
General Editor

Facts On File
An Infobase Learning Company

Student Handbook to Psychology: Developmental Psychology
Copyright © 2012 Lynn M. Shelley

Facts On File, Inc.
An Imprint of Infobase Learning
132 West 31st Street
New York NY 10001

Library of Congress Cataloging-in-Publication Data
Student handbook to psychology / [edited by] Bernard C. Beins.
    v. ; cm.
Includes bibliographical references and index.
    Contents: v. 1. History, perspectives, and applications / Kenneth D. Keith—v. 2. Methods and measurements / Bernard C. Beins—v. 3. Brain and mind / Michael Kerchner—v. 4. Learning and thinking / Christopher M. Hakala and Bernard C. Beins—v. 5. Developmental psychology / Lynn Shelley—v. 6. Personality and abnormal psychology / Janet F. Carlson—v. 7. Social psychology / Jeffrey D. Holmes and Sheila K. Singh.
    ISBN 978-0-8160-8280-3 (set : alk. paper)—ISBN 978-0-8160-8281-0 (v. 1 : alk. paper)—ISBN 978-0-8160-8286-5 (v. 2 : alk. paper)—ISBN 978-0-8160-8285-8 (v. 3 : alk. paper)—ISBN 978-0-8160-8284-1 (v. 4 : alk. paper)—ISBN 978-0-8160-8282-7 (v. 5 : alk. paper)—ISBN 978-0-8160-8287-2 (v. 6 : alk. paper)—ISBN 978-0-8160-8283-4 (v. 7 : alk. paper) 1. Psychology—Textbooks.
I. Beins, Bernard.
    BF121.S884 2012
    150—dc23   2011045277

Facts On File books are available at special discounts when purchased in bulk quantities for businesses, associations, institutions, or sales promotions. Please call our Special Sales Department in New York at (212) 967-8800 or (800) 322-8755.

You can find Facts On File on the World Wide Web at http://www.infobaselearning.com

Text design by Erika K. Arroyo
Cover design by Takeshi Takahashi
Composition by EJB Publishing Services
Cover printed by Yurchak Printing, Landisville, Pa.
Book printed and bound by Yurchak Printing, Landisville, Pa.
Date printed: September 2012
Printed in the United States of America

This book is printed on acid-free paper.

CONTENTS

PREFACE

Behavior is endlessly fascinating. People and other animals are complicated creatures that show extraordinary patterns of abilities, intelligence, social interaction, and creativity along with, unfortunately, problematic behaviors. All of these characteristics emerge because of the way the brain interprets incoming information and directs our responses to that information.

This seven-volume **Student Handbook to Psychology** set highlights important and interesting facets of thought and behavior. It provides a solid foundation for learning about psychological processes associated with growth and development, social issues, thinking and problem solving, and abnormal thought and behavior. Most of the major schools and theories related to psychology appear in the books in the series, albeit in abbreviated form. Because psychology is such a highly complex and diverse discipline, these volumes present a broad overview of the subject rather than a complete and definitive treatise. Such a work, in fact, would be difficult (if not impossible) because psychological scientists are still searching for answers to a great number of questions. If you are interested in delving in more depth into specific areas of psychology, we have provided a bibliography of accessible readings to help you fill in the details.

The volumes in this series follow the order that you might see in a standard presentation on a variety of topics, but each book stands alone and the series does not need to be read in any particular order. In fact, you can peruse individual chapters in each volume at will, seeking out and focusing on those topics that interest you most. On the other hand, if you do choose to read through a complete volume, you will find a flow of information that connects related sections of the books, providing a coherent overview of the entire discipline of psychology.

The authors of the seven volumes in this series are experts in their respective fields, so you will find psychological concepts that are up to date and that reflect the most recent advances in scientific knowledge about thought and behavior. In addition, each of the authors is an excellent writer who has presented the information in an interesting and compelling fashion. Although some of the material and many of the ideas are complex, the authors have done an outstanding job of conveying those ideas in ways that are both interesting and effective.

In *History, Perspectives, and Applications*, Professor Kenneth Keith of the University of San Diego has woven historical details into a tapestry that shows how psychological questions originated within a philosophical framework, incorporated biological concepts, and ultimately evolved into a single scientific discipline that remains interconnected with many other academic and scientific disciplines. Dr. Keith has identified the major figures associated with the development of the field of psychology as well as the social forces that helped shape their ideas.

In *Methods and Measurements*, I illustrate how psychologists create new knowledge through research. The volume presents the major approaches to research and explains how psychologists develop approaches to research that help us answer questions about complex aspects of behavior. Without these well-structured and proven research methods, we would not have much of the information we now have about behavior. Furthermore, these methods, approaches, and practices provide confidence that the knowledge we do have is good knowledge, grounded in solid research.

Many people are under the impression that each thought or behavior is a single thing. In *Brain and Mind*, Professor Michael Kerchner of Washington College dispels this impression by showing how the myriad structures and functions of our brain work in unison to create those seemingly simple and one-dimensional behaviors. As the author explains, each behavior is really the result of many different parts of the brain engaging in effective communication with one another. Professor Kerchner also explains what occurs when this integration breaks down.

Learning and Thinking, co-authored by Professor Christopher Hakala of Western New England College and me (at Ithaca College), explores the fascinating field of cognitive psychology, a discipline focused on the processes by which people learn, solve problems, and display intelligence. Cognitive psychology is a fascinating field that explores how we absorb information, integrate it, and then act on it.

In *Developmental Psychology*, Professor Lynn Shelley of Westfield State University addresses the very broad area of psychology that examines how people develop and change from the moment of conception through old age. Dr. Shelley's detailed and compelling explanation includes a focus on how maturation and environment play a part in shaping how each individual grows, evolves, and changes.

In *Personality and Abnormal Psychology*, Professor Janet Carlson of the Buros Center for Testing at the University of Nebraska (Lincoln) addresses various dimensions of personality, highlighting processes that influence normal and abnormal facets of personality. Dr. Carlson also explains how psychologists study the fundamental nature of personality and how it unfolds.

The final volume in this series is *Social Psychology*. Co-authored by Professor Jeffrey Holmes of Ithaca College and Sheila Singh of Cornell University, this volume examines how our thoughts and behaviors emerge in connection with our interactions with other people. As the authors of this volume explain, changes in a person's social environment can lead to notable changes in the way that person thinks and behaves.

As editor of this series, I have had the opportunity to work with all of the authors who have contributed their expertise and insights to this project. During this collaborative process, I found that we have much in common. All of us have spent our careers pondering why people think and act the way they do. For every answer we come up with, we also develop new questions that are just as interesting and important. And we all agree that you cannot find a more interesting subject to study than psychology.

As you learn about psychology, we hope that the information in these seven volumes inspires the same fascination in you. We also hope that our explanations, illustrations, and narrative studies motivate you to continue studying why we humans are the way we are.

—Bernard C. Beins, Ph.D., Professor of Psychology,
Ithaca College, Series Editor

CHAPTER 1

THE SCIENTIFIC STUDY OF HUMAN DEVELOPMENT

Welcome to the scientific study of human development. Throughout this chapter new terms from the developmental sciences will be presented. How developmental psychology is related to other areas of study will be discussed, and key issues in the field will be explored. The history of developmental psychology and its driving theories will be described, followed by a review of how to conduct developmental research. Each chapter features sidebars and vignettes with a vignette that highlights some of the major concepts presented.

The social scientists, educators, medical professionals, and clinicians who study human development are called **developmentalists**. The field of developmental science is multidisciplinary, meaning that scientists from many different backgrounds are engaged in this study of human development. Together, their various perspectives give us a thorough understanding of the complexities of the field, one of many fields that comprise the discipline of psychology. Because this volume is part of a series of psychology books, we will begin by defining what **psychology** is.

When students are asked to share words or phrases that belong in the definition of **psychology**, they typically begin with the phrase "study of" and add words like "humans," "mind," "personality," "perception," and "cognition." Very few come up with the word "scientific." Different psychologists will use somewhat varied terminology, including words like "personality," "interpersonal," "mental processes," or "unconscious," but all include the word "scientific" in their definitions. A good, simple definition of psychology is *the scientific study*

Thomas

Thomas was born the second child of Kim and Elliot. He was a happy and active baby. Like many babies, Thomas had a lot of ear infections. He walked early and talked late. In fact, at three years old he grunted more than he talked. The pediatrician said his language delay was due to the ear infections. As a toddler, Thomas had a "reputation." He constantly fought with other children, especially his sister. His grandparents joked that he was going to end up in jail. They said Elliot and Kim needed to "beat some sense into him." His pre-school teacher told them, "he's psychotic." But the pediatrician said Thomas was normal.

In kindergarten, Thomas rarely sat in his seat; he spent the day wandering around, or wound up in trouble for bothering other kids. He was never called on, never chosen as teacher's helper, and often excluded from activities as pun-ishment for bad behavior. Kim worried that he wasn't learning, and requested extra help from the school. The response was, "He's still young, and he's a boy, you need to wait to see what happens." Thomas repeated kindergarten.

At home there was constant bickering between Thomas and his sister. His father blamed everything on Kim. He said she was a bad mother who could not control her children. Bickering and yelling went on between everyone—Thomas and his sister, Thomas and Kim, Thomas and Elliot, and especially Elliot and Kim. Soon Elliot moved out, and after a messy court battle the couple divorced.

By the time Thomas was 7, his behavior had gotten so aggressive that his sister was regularly injured. The family's pediatrician finally suggested they see a child psychiatrist who immediately determined Thomas had severe prob-lems and had him admitted to a hospital for two weeks. While in the hospital, Thomas was diagnosed with Attention Deficit Hyperactivity Disorder (ADHD). At the advice of the psychiatrist, Kim read everything she could find about ADHD and behavioral treatments. She took classes in behavioral therapy, and learned how to keep charts and use rewards and consequences in response to Thomas' behavior. Thomas was placed on medication and began regular behavioral therapy. His behavior improved dramatically, and family life became peaceful and harmonious. People stopped telling Kim she was a bad mother, and Thomas' grandparents stopped saying he would end up in jail—sometimes they even said he would end up president.

Thomas' story is not unusual. His mother sought the guidance of "experts." Some were very helpful, and some seemed to lack an understanding of typical child development. Some based their advice on personal opinions, and others used theory and science as a basis for their advice. At the end of this chapter, you'll learn more about what happened to Thomas after he was diagnosed.

of the human mind, behavior, and emotions, with the most important part of this definition centered in the word "scientific."

In most libraries, psychology books are all located on shelves in the BF section. The BF books are far away from books covering the field of medicine (R) and psychiatry (RC); they are also far away from Education (L), physiology (QP), and sociology (HM). The psychology books (BF), however, are right next to philosophy books (B). Why? To answer this question, one needs to know a little about what philosophers do and a little about how that is related to what psychologists do. Historically, philosophers have used their intellect to study and explain the reasons for and causes of phenomenon, often using logical reasoning to explain phenomenon related to humans. And this is precisely what the earliest psychologists did. They thought about human behaviors and then derived sets of ideas to explain and sometimes predict those behaviors. Just like philosophers, they developed theories. A **theory** is a set of ideas used to explain some phenomenon.

Psychology emerged into its own distinct field of study, when psychologists began to scientifically test the theories put forward by philosophers. So, the main distinction between the field of psychology and the field of philosophy is **empiricism**. Philosophers rely on their intellect to discover "truths," whereas psychologists begin with a theoretical explanation for something, and then test that theory using empirical research. Something is empirical if it is based on observable experiences, experimentation or data.

So a true psychologist explaining some phenomenon will base her or his assertions on science . . . not on logic, morality, ethics, or religion (even though religion books sit just to the right of the psychology books in the library, in the BL section). The difference between true and not so true pop psychology can be clearly seen and heard on popular television and radio broadcasts. Good media psychologists recognize that psychologists use theory and science to guide their thinking and assertions and adhere to this principle. Not so good ones don't. So if the television or radio "psychologist" is spouting personal opinions, making value statements such as "one should" or "ought to," or claiming to know "truths" or "able to prove" something, he or she is not behaving like a psychologist and is most likely not a true psychologist.

DEVELOPMENTAL PSYCHOLOGY

From the basic understanding and definition of psychology presented above, we can take the next important step and define **developmental psychology**. This is rather easy. We begin with our original definition of psychology—*the scientific study of the human mind, behavior, and emotions*—and add the phrase *and how they change over time.* The newly added phrase refines the basic definition of psychology by adding information that we more or less intuitively know—that an individual is very different at 5, 10, 20, and 30 years of age. Certainly there are physical differences, such as height and weight. But there are also social and cognitive differences. At different life stages one thinks about the world differently, deals with emotions differently, struggles with different psychological tasks or crises, and interacts with others differently. Each of these differences depends upon a whole host of variables related to time such as chronological age, maturity, and countless prior experiences. And all of this, in essence, is what will be explored in this book. Humans change over time, and this volume takes a chronological approach to our consideration of those changes—from conception to death or, in the parlance of psychologists, *from sperm to worm.*

An Interdisciplinary Science
Every psychologist probably believes that his or her area of expertise is the most important area of psychology, but in the instance of developmental psychology, it is true. Why? Because, every other area of psychology is interested in some aspect of human development. A corollary to this is that you will find mention of every other area of psychology in every developmental psychology textbook. Moreover, many fields of study outside the discipline of psychology require an understanding of human development. It is for this reason that future educators, social workers, police officers, and medical professionals are all required to take classes in developmental psychology. In addition, many professional developmentalists serve as consultants to youth leaders, educators, nurses, doctors, physical and occupational therapists, neuroscientists, religious leaders, sociologists, geneticists, public policy makers, criminal justice workers, marketers, counselors, and clinicians. All of this makes it rather apparent that anybody working with humans wants (or at least needs) to better understand human development. And all of this also underscores that the field of developmental science is **interdisciplinary**.

The theory and research presented in this book come from many fields of study, including neuroscience, education, medicine, sociology, anthropology, and psychology. Theories and methodologies from these various fields often combine to create new theories and research studies. However, developmentalists do not usually study large populations, as do sociologists or anthropologists; they are interested in individual differences.

Unique Individuals
Developmentalists are interested in how humans change over time, therefore they study individuals from every age group. They are in fact interested in all types of people—all ages; all ethnic and cultural backgrounds; the rich, poor, and everyone in between; those who are able bodied, as well as those who live with a disabling condition; and even people from different historical time periods.

Developmentalists are interested in how factors, such as age, culture, history, and life experiences impact the individual. *(Shutterstock)*

Developmentalists study the individual, not the group. The underlying goal is to better understand how the unique background and life experiences of an individual impact her or his developmental pathway. One important aspect of this goal is to understand that the background and life experiences of each individual all occur within a greater context.

Context

Most people agree that understanding a child's development means looking at how the parents treat that child. However, developmental scientists also look beyond the child's immediate family and adopt an **ecological perspective**. This perspective proposes that scientists look at all of the contexts in which development occurs (Bronfenbrenner, 1977). Neighborhood, school, family, friends, and religious institutions are all aspects of this context. So are governmental policies, system of government, media, historical time period, cultural background, and economic status. When considering this broad array of environmental agents, it is easy to see that context has a tremendous impact on development.

Often these various contextual layers interact and influence each other. For example, seven-year-old Thomas was having a difficult time reading in school. To understand why, and how to help him, we need to look at many layers of influence. First, Thomas' father spent very little time with him, and this upset Thomas. As custodial parent, his mother was often exhausted from full-time work, so she did not have much time to read with him. She noticed that Thomas did not know the sounds of letters and asked his teacher to pay special attention to him. The teacher replied that the financial situation of the city had resulted in budget cuts in the school, which meant she had a large class of 30 children and could only hold group reading lessons. The after-school program Thomas attended at the YMCA noticed his reading difficulties, but the program was not staffed by trained educators so the people working there usually just read aloud to him. National government policies would require Thomas be assessed if his parents requested it, and for the school to provide remediation if necessary. But his mother was unaware of these laws, so she did not demand testing.

In this example, Thomas' classroom reading instruction was inadequate, but there were many other factors influencing the problem, ranging from an uninvolved father to budget cuts and national education policies. Even though some of these contexts did not directly involve Thomas, it is clear that they all influenced his development.

Nature-Nurture

As mentioned earlier in this chapter, the field of American psychology emerged from the discipline of philosophy. One of the earliest philosophical debates developmentalists struggled with, and continue to struggle with, is the nature-nurture debate. This debate revolves around a single question: Which has more influence on human development, nature or nurture?

The terms nature and nurture can be confusing. Some students mistakenly think "nature" includes trees, grass, and bushes, so that must mean environmental influences, or context. This is definitely not the case. **Nature** refers to everything that comes with us when we enter the world at birth. The nature position asserts that our biological make-up and genetic components are the primary influence on human growth and development. In contrast, **nurture** is the way we are raised; it includes all of the experiences we have had while interacting with the outside world.

The nature-nurture debate often pops up when we try to determine the cause of something. For example, attention deficit hyperactivity disorder (ADHD) makes it difficult for children to inhibit their spontaneous responses—responses that can involve everything from movement to speech and attentiveness. Parents often wonder if ADHD is due to nature (biology) or nurture (the way the child was raised). This is a difficult and complicated question to answer, and part of the difficulty arises from the fact that nature-nurture questions can rarely be answered clearly and definitively as one or the other. For example, there is growing evidence that in children with ADHD, some parts of the brain develop at a slower rate in children with ADHD than in the brains of children without ADHD. In fact many mothers report that their ADHD-affected children were overactive even while in the womb. This evidence clearly supports the argument that ADHD is a biological condition and is part of the nature of the individual.

However, a number of research reports also show that on average parents of children with ADHD use more harsh discipline, have high levels of stress, and are more likely themselves to have had a psychiatric diagnosis. In fact, a number of studies have demonstrated that after parents are trained to use more effective parenting strategies, their children exhibit lower rates of problematic behaviors associated with ADHD. These findings support the argument that ADHD symptoms are (at least partially) caused by nurturing.

So, is ADHD caused by nature (in this case, brain differences) or nurture (ineffective parenting strategies)? Taken together, these findings suggest that there is no clear answer. In fact, it looks like there is an interaction between nature and nurture. Perhaps children with ADHD are born with brains that develop at a different rate than their peers, leaving them with slightly lower than average ability to focus and slightly greater than average activity levels. And perhaps these slight differences become exaggerated when parents become stressed and impatient when trying to discipline and nurture their children. As a result of the stress related to parenting a child with ADHD, the parents may use harsh discipline, and the final result are children who show tremendous differences in activity and attention. If this is true, both nature and nurture are influential and both seem to play an important role in ADHD. Moreover, the influence is multidirectional, with the interplay between nature and nurture sometimes exacerbating the condition.

Multidirectional Influences

Multidirectional influences occur when the individual influences the environment, and that environment in turn influences the individual. The birth of a child certainly influences the environment into which she or he is born. For example, because newborns cannot care for themselves, new parents spend most of the day caring for their baby. They get little sleep and have almost no time for their own school or work, often causing them to be impatient with the baby. When parents are impatient babies get fussy and demand even more attention. So each influences the other, there is a back-and-forth.

But the back and forth influence does not only happen with nurturing. Nature influences nurture, which influences nature, which influences nurture. For example, even before being born, the child is influenced by the environment of his or her mother. For example, when a pregnant mother has very little food, lives in a place impacted by environmental hazards (such as lead and other pollutants), and must deliver her baby without the assistance of a trained attendant, that baby is at higher risk for biological problems such as malnutrition and brain damage. In contrast, a child born to a mother who has access to healthy foods, fresh air, and good medical attention is much more likely to be born healthy. So the biological make-up of the child is influenced by the environment long before the child is even born. In turn, the health of the newborn baby will influence the type of care he or she receives from parents and medical professionals.

HISTORY AND THEORY

Today the field of developmental psychology emphasizes the importance of understanding context, multidirectional influence, and both typical and atypical development. However, trends in what psychologists study have been influenced both by history and culture. The developmental theories of early philosophers were often based on the spiritual teachings of their times. Some argued in support of the Christian doctrine of **original sin**, which views children as innately selfish until parents teach them otherwise. Others, such as Swiss philosopher *Jean-Jacques Rousseau* (1712–1778) proposed children are innately good and simply need nurturing to reach their full potential. Both positions argued that there is a struggle between internal and external forces, or nature and nurture.

It is difficult to know exactly when the scientific study of human development broke away from philosophy; however, the late 19th century saw the beginnings of a proliferation of theories. The **evolutionary theory** of British naturalist, *Charles Darwin* (1809–1882) is usually credited as being the foundation for a number of developmental theories. Darwin emphasized **natural selection** and the idea that those species or individuals best equipped to meet the demands of the environment survive long enough to reproduce, whereas those less suited to the environment die off. Like Darwin, Americans *G. Stanley Hall* (1844–1924) and his student *Arnold Gesell* (1880–1961) also viewed development as a **maturational process.**

Beginning at the start of the 20th century, a variety of theories emerged, each attempting to explain just about every aspect of human development. The **psychoanalytic theories** attempted to explain individual differences in personality. Led by Viennese physician, *Sigmund Freud* (1856–1939), psychoanalysts proposed that people move through a series of stages; at each stage they confront a conflict between internal biological drives and external societal expectations. Freud's **psychosexual stages** emphasized a child's sexual drives, and the role parents play in permitting or limiting the gratification of those drives. Similarly, a follower of Freud's, *Erik Erikson* (1902–1994), proposed *psychoso-*

cial stages that also recognized unconscious forces but placed more emphasis on social or cultural demands. Psychoanalytic theories placed an important emphasis on the role of early childhood experiences; however, they were also vague and difficult to test empirically.

In contrast, **behavioral theorists** studied directly observable events. In 1906 Russian physiologist *Ivan Pavlov* (1849–1936) first published the results of his studies on **classical conditioning**. Pavlov's studies involved training a dog to salivate at the sound of a bell. In 1920, in an attempt to demonstrate classical conditioning in a human, American *John Watson* (1878–1958) attempted to condition a boy known as "Little Albert" to fear a neutral stimulus by making a loud noise every time the 11-month-old Albert was near a soft white rat. Albert supposedly learned to fear the rat, and Watson argued that environment, and not internal drives, was the main influence on development. Another behaviorist, *B.F. Skinner* (1904–1990) used **reinforcement** to increase desirable behaviors, and **punishment** to decrease undesirable behaviors. Principles based on these theories have been widely used to treat a number of behavior problems, such as the problem behaviors exhibited by Thomas described at the beginning of this chapter; however, behavioral theories have been criticized for narrowly focusing on immediate environmental influences and largely ignoring the influence of unobservable factors such as thoughts or emotions.

Cognitive theories emphasize developmental changes in mental processes, such as logic, memory, and language development. By far, the most influential cognitive theorist was Swiss developmentalist *Jean Piaget* (1896–1980). Like Darwin, Piaget was interested in the biological concept of adaptation. He proposed that mental structures adapt to meet the demands of the environment, and he viewed children as active learners who move through four stages of cognitive development. A more contemporary theory is **information processing**. This theoretical approach also views children as active learners, but emphasizes how the mind manages and organizes information.

Of course there are many more theories of human development, and both scientific advances and historical issues influence trends in theoretical writings and empirical research. For example, contemporary advances in brain research and genetics have influenced modern biological theories. The major theoretical approaches described in this chapter focus on different domains of development, and each theory has its own strengths and weaknesses. Today's psychologists often adopt an **eclectic** perspective, using multiple theoretical approaches to explain human development. Psychoanalytic, behavioral, cognitive, and biological theories will be presented in more detail throughout this book.

CONDUCTING RESEARCH

As noted at the start of this chapter, theories are one important aspect of developmental science; the other important aspect is research. Because developmentalists are curious about so many different aspects of development, it is difficult to design and conduct one research study that addresses everything of interest. In fact, it is impossible for one study to do it all. Human beings and the environments in which they live are just too complex. That is why developmentalists draw conclusions based on numerous studies conducted with slightly different methods, at different points in time, and on different groups of people. One unique aspect of developmental research is that it usually includes a variable that measures time.

Developmental Research

Developmental research looks at how individuals change or develop over time. Therefore, in most developmental studies, an important variable is age, or time. Scientists use several different research designs to study human development: longitudinal, cross-sectional, or sequential.

Longitudinal research follows the same individuals over a long period of time. For example, the New York Longitudinal Study (NYLS) conducted by Stella Chess and Alexander Thomas lasted for decades. The first wave of data collection began in 1956 and followed 185 children from infancy to 7 or 8 years of age. The study rated infants on a number of behavioral characteristics and collected an enormous amount of data on parent and child behaviors. The researchers identified nine temperamental characteristics, such as level of physical activity and distractibility. **Temperament** refers to personality predispositions that are present at birth and assumed to be inborn, or innate. Chess and Thomas concluded that the goal should be a "good fit" between parenting behaviors and the child's temperament.

Longitudinal studies such as the NYLS gather a lot of information about one group of individuals over a long period of time, so we learn a great deal about how that group develops. But, there are limitations with this type of design. First, because the study takes so long, some people drop out. Some move away, others lose interest. Some stop participating because of illness, and others die. When participants leave the study before it is done it is called **mortality** or **attrition**. This means the researcher had more participants at the start of the study than at the end. If participants randomly drop out, this might not be a problem. It can however be a big problem if one type of participant is more likely to drop out than others. Suppose for example that parents with more challenging children found keeping appointments for the NYLS too challenging and disproportionately dropped out. This would result in very

Revisiting Thomas

After 7-year-old Thomas was diagnosed with ADHD, a therapist taught his mother, Kim, to use behavioral techniques where rewards are given for good behaviors and consequences given for bad behaviors. Thomas responded well. His father Elliot continued to deny Thomas had a problem. He refused to learn the behavioral techniques, and when Thomas spent time with his father they argued almost non-stop. They gradually spent less and less time together.

Kim wanted the school to use behavioral techniques so she met with Thomas's teacher and principal. During these meetings she explained behavioral therapy. The principal was uninterested, but the first grade teacher listened and began using charts with stickers for rewards and consequences. Thomas's behavior in the classroom improved dramatically. But three months later Thomas hit another child on the playground. A playground aid told him he would not have recess the next day. Thomas thought this was unfair. In the classroom, he was distraught and continued to express unhappiness with the punishment. The teacher sent him to the principal's office to calm down, but he refused to go. Soon the principal and school psychologist came into the classroom and physically dragged Thomas to the office. This angered Thomas even more and he rolled on the floor kicking and biting people. As adults continued to try to physically control him, his behavior got more aggressive. The police were called. By the time they arrived Thomas had settled down, but they still had a firm talk with him and he spent the rest of the day in a "time-out" room alone. When Kim arrived to pick him up at the end of the day, the principal told her about the incident, adding that Thomas was suspended from school for one week.

Kim was furious. She asked why behavioral techniques had not been used. The principal said she didn't know anything about behavioral techniques. Kim asked why she wasn't called sooner. The principal said she thought Kim would not want to be bothered at work.

Kim began to educate herself about special education laws. She fought the school to get Thomas tested, and it was found that in addition to ADHD, he had a learning disability. He began spending part of his day with a reading specialist in a resource room. His academics and behavior both improved. Eventually his father educated himself about ADHD and began to comply with Thomas' treatment program. By the end of second grade Thomas was no longer the child creating problems; instead, he was the kid helping other kids. This story has a happy ending, but only because Thomas's mother worked long and hard to get the services her son needed.

few "difficult" children in the study, a situation that would make it appear as if "difficulty" were an uncommon temperament classification.

Another problem with longitudinal studies is that the cohort studied may not represent other cohorts. A **cohort** is a group of individuals who share something in common—in longitudinal studies, this is usually age. For example, parenting advice for children born in 1956 was very different from parenting advice given for children born today. In 1956 it was rare for fathers to be present at the birth of their children or for mothers to be alert during the delivery. Hence, perhaps because of these and similar differences the results of the NYLS do not **generalize**, or apply, to children born today.

Cross-sectional research is much quicker to conduct than longitudinal research, and solves some of the limitations associated with longitudinal research design. Cross-sectional studies examine many different age groups at one time. For example, to study developmental changes in activity level we might look at four groups of children of different ages, such as groups of 4-, 6-, 8- and 10-year-olds. If we find that the younger groups are significantly more active than the older groups, we might conclude that activity level decreases with age. Cross-sectional studies such as this one are quick to do, but the researcher is never sure the individuals in the youngest age group will grow up to behave like the individuals in the oldest age group. It is inferred that this will happen, but perhaps there was something unique about one or some of the age groups, or cohorts. The observed differences might be due to one age group experiencing different parenting, or teaching. Nonetheless, this is a good design for some research questions.

Sequential research is a combination of longitudinal and cross-sectional methods, and addresses the weaknesses of both research designs. In sequential studies the same individuals are studied over time, however at the beginning of the study there are a number of different age groups. This means that the entire length of the study can be shorter than a longitudinal study, and the researchers still obtain information about all ages of interest. For example, a study done by researchers from the National Institute of Mental Health and McGill University looked at the brains of 446 participants who ranged in age from four years old to young adulthood. The researchers used brain scans that were taken on at least two occasions three years apart, and it took about 7 years to collect all of the data (this is much shorter than following 4-year-olds all the way into adulthood). At the beginning of the study half of the participants had ADHD. What the researchers found is that in the children with ADHD parts of their brains developed and thickened on average when the child was 10.5 years old; in children without ADHD, this occurred earlier (on average at 7.5 years of age). These delayed physical changes to the brain meant that children with ADHD developed the ability to control their impulses, focus their attention, and control their body movements later than their non-ADHD peers.

A sequential design such as this allows for comparisons between cohorts—if the behavior of different cohorts at the same age differs, the researcher knows there is a **cohort effect**. On the other hand, if the same developmental pattern is found in two cohorts, there is stronger evidence than can be concluded from using only a cross-sectional or a longitudinal study.

Tables 1.1, 1.2, and 1.3 illustrate longitudinal, cross-sectional, and sequential studies, respectively. In the sequential study, you can examine cohort effects by comparing cohort 2 in 2012 to cohort 1 in 2014, and cohort 3 in 2014 to cohort 2 in 2016.

TABLE 1.1
Longitudinal Study

Year Studied	2012	2014	2016	2018	2020
Cohort 1	4 years old	6 years old	8 years old	10 years old	12 years old

TABLE 1.2
Cross-Sectional Study

Year Studied	2014
Cohort 1	4 years old
Cohort 2	6 years old
Cohort 3	8 years old
Cohort 4	12 years old

TABLE 1.3
Sequential

Year Studied	2012	2014	2016
Cohort 1	4 years old	6 years old	8 years old
Cohort 2	6 years old	8 years old	10 years old
Cohort 3	8 years old	10 years old	12 years old

CONCLUSION

Developmentalists are interested in the scientific study of the human mind, behavior, and emotions and how they change over time. They are also interested in how context influences development. Today, the field of developmental science is interdisciplinary. However, many of the earliest developmentalists were philosophers who pondered questions such as "Which is more influential on human development, nature or nurture?" Today's developmentalists are social scientists who are interested both in theory and in empirical research. Theories guide the research questions posed, empirical research tests the premises of the theories, and research ultimately leads to new areas of inquiry and theory development. To study *development,* researchers look at individuals at various points in time or individuals of different ages. There are a number of challenges to conducting this type of research, and it is important to be aware of these challenges when designing developmental studies and when interpreting the results from developmental studies.

Further Reading

American Academy of Pediatrics. Available at http://www.aap.org/.
Children's Defense Fund. Available at http://www.childrensdefense.org/.
Harder, Arlene F. "The Developmental Stages of Erik Erikson." [article on-line]. Accessed August 1, 2011; available from http://www.learningplaceonline.com/stages/organize/Erikson.htm.

CHAPTER 2

PRENATAL DEVELOPMENT AND BIRTH

This chapter follows the course of prenatal development, exploring protective steps that can help insure a healthy pregnancy as well as potential risks and threats to the unborn child. Childbirth is described, along with the medical procedures that potentially help or hinder the birth process. The chapter concludes with a description of the typical newborn baby, and with some of the issues associated with babies born too soon or too small.

All humans begin as a single cell. An egg and sperm unite to form that single cell, and that single cell is now an organism that begins to grow inside a woman. While she walks around, talks, eats, laughs, works, cries, and loves, that organism continues to grow until the woman delivers a baby from her body. For most women and children, most of the time, the entire process goes smoothly. It is a miracle.

PRENATAL DEVELOPMENT

When the egg, also called an **ovum**, and sperm unite, it is called **fertilization** or conception, and the resulting organism is called a **zygote**. Half of the genetic information for this organism is from the egg; the other half is from the sperm. Look at the incredible picture of the egg and sperm uniting. Notice that the egg is much larger than the sperm. In fact, it is about 10,000 times larger. The sperm has only one job—to deliver genetic information to the egg. Notice that the sperm consists of a tail that makes movement fast and efficient, a body, and a head that contains the genetic information. In contrast, the egg contains genetic

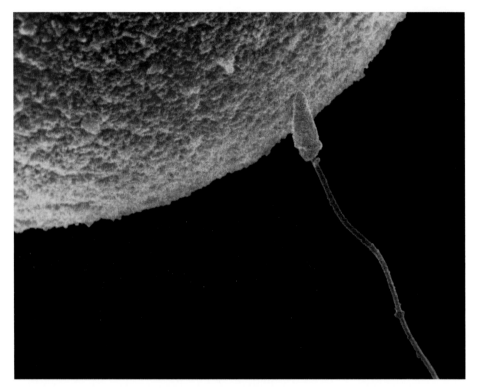

Egg and sperm unite to form a human cell. *(Shutterstock)*

information, but it also comes prepared to support the growth of the zygote. The egg contains a large store of nutrients to nourish the developing organism until it can rely on nourishment from the mother's body. This allows the developing organism to grow even before the umbilical cord becomes a source of nourishment around the fifth week after conception.

Scientists divide pregnancy into three distinct periods; the germinal period, the embryonic period, and the fetal period. The following section will describe these three periods.

The Germinal Period

Fertilization usually occurs in one of the woman's fallopian tubes. The zygote travels down the fallopian tube, and as it travels it begins the process of duplicating itself, and then dividing. The new cells continue to do this several times. They make exact copies of themselves and then divide. Eventually they form a ball, with an inner layer of cells (that will ultimately be the fetus) and an outer layer (that will eventually be the support structures such as the amniotic sac and placenta). During these first few cell divisions, all of the cells are exactly the same—they are undifferentiated.

Stem Cells

Undifferentiated cells are also called stem cells, and the subject of stem cell research is often in the news. The neat thing about stem cells is that they have the potential to become any type of cell in the body. This is special because most cells can be only one thing. A skin cell can only develop into a skin cell, and a brain cell can be nothing but a brain cell. But stem cells can go on to be any type of cell. Scientists believe a better understanding of stem cells will lead to new treatments for diseases that are caused by problems with differentiation, for example, cancer and some birth defects. They also believe if they learn more about stem cells they will be able to form cells and tissues that can be used to replace damaged cells or tissues.

Where do researchers get stem cells for their research? There are three main sources: adult cells taken from an adult's bone marrow during a painful procedure, cord cells that are available from a baby's umbilical cord after delivery, or embryonic cells. Sometimes, when a couple uses assisted reproductive technology (ART) to get pregnant, several eggs are removed from the woman's body, and those eggs are fertilized outside of her body. A small number of fertilized eggs are then placed back into the woman to grow. Often there are extra fertilized eggs, and sometimes couples decide to donate them for scientific research. Some people say using these stem cells for research is the same as taking a life, and they want this practice to be illegal. Knowledge about prenatal development enables people to form their own opinion about this controversial subject.

After the cells have duplicated and divided several times they will become **differentiated**, or specialized. While this is happening, the zygote is traveling down the fallopian tube and into the uterus. Once in the uterus, it will find a place to attach itself to the thick, rich uterine lining. This is called **implantation**. It is at this time that a woman can take a home pregnancy test and get a fairly accurate result. Before this, pregnancy test results are unreliable.

The first two weeks of pregnancy, from fertilization to implantation, are called the **germinal period**. This is a fairly risky time—some researchers estimate that up to 80 percent of fertilized eggs fail to implant. During this two-week time frame, most women are not aware conception has occurred. Their period comes on time, or a little late, and unless they have used assisted reproductive technologies (ART) they have no way of knowing they may have conceived.

The Embryonic Period

The developing organism is now called an **embryo**. The period of the embryo begins at implantation and lasts through the eighth week of pregnancy. It is a

Emmanuel and Seya

Emmanuel Makanza is a 30-year-old farmer who grows maize, sorghum, and millet on a small plot of land on the outskirts of Berega, Tanzania. He lives 8 miles from the nearest paved road and 30 miles from the last electric pole. His 28-year-old wife Seya is pregnant. They already have two daughters. This is her fourth pregnancy. Her previous pregnancy ended badly. Labor came early and quickly. Emmanuel and his mother-in-law were with Seya. Remembering that day, he says "I know there is no pain relief. It hurts. Women know this and are designed to bear it. It is a sign of honor when they do it alone. But there were problems. At first we thought she should give birth at home, but I changed my mind." After 36 hours of labor Emmanuel put his wife on a bike and cycled her to a health center an hour away. The health center was a small mud hut, stocked with no drugs, little equipment, and no running water. A trained midwife was present and assisted with the delivery. Seya survived, but their son did not.

Now Seya is nearing the end of pregnancy again. After her last pregnancy, she and her children received several immunizations. But other than that she has had no medical care since her last delivery. When asked about the developing life inside of Seya, Emmanuel says, "It is a miracle. It is impossible to know what is happening inside her." Seya agrees. "I don't think about a baby inside me. I don't know what is happening to it at different times in the pregnancy. I don't know why one survives and another doesn't. I'm too tired to think about it."

It is not surprising Seya feels tired. At first light she wakes up and walks a half mile to fetch water. She makes breakfast, cleans her house, and then leaves her daughters home alone so she can work in the fields with Emmanuel. At the end of the day she returns home to cook dinner and go to bed. "If I stop, how will we survive?" she asks. Emmanuel also worries about getting work done without Seya's help, but he is more worried about Seya giving birth. With only a few weeks until the delivery, he and Seya decide she will move in with Emmanuel's brother who lives closer to the health center. Emmanuel says, "Life is a gift from God. Her body knows how to do it. We just need to help as best we can."

Seya happily proclaims, "I can't wait to give birth. I will get three weeks off from collecting water, and I won't go back to the hot field for three months. I can be with my children." But, while she is away, and even after her return, their 7- and 5-year-old daughters will take on all responsibilities for water, cooking, and cleaning.

Every year, approximately 13,000 Tanzanian women die as a result of pregnancy or childbirth related problems. Tanzania is one of the world's poorest countries, and its rate of maternal death is one of the highest in the world. Few health workers, shortages in drugs, and little equipment combined with cultural attitudes that encourage home births are the main causes for the high rates of risk.

time of incredibly rapid growth. The foundation is laid for all of the organ systems. By the end of this period the embryo has the beginnings of all major body structures, including the eyes, nose, arms, fingers, legs, and internal organs, such as the heart, liver, and spleen.

At the start of the embryonic period, the **neural tube** also forms. The neural tube will eventually become the spinal cord and brain, but for now, it is the site where neurons (or nerve cells) are formed before traveling to their final destination. By the end of this period, the embryo can move and respond to touch, yet it is only about 1 inch long and weighs half an ounce. Despite its ability to move, the mother still cannot feel the embryo inside of her.

The Fetal Period

The longest prenatal period is the period of the **fetus**, which lasts from the ninth week of pregnancy until the end of the pregnancy. Growth continues, and the organ systems become fully developed.

Sometimes pregnant women talk about the length of pregnancy in terms of *trimesters*. This terminology is used when pregnancy is divided into three equal parts. The first trimester includes the germinal, embryonic, and the first month of the fetal periods. By the end of the first trimester the nervous system is slowly becoming organized, the lungs will expand and contract rhythmically mimicking breathing, and the fetus shows various facial expressions.

In the second trimester, the mother will be able to feel the fetus move around. Inside the womb the fetus is covered in a white substance called **vernix**, which protects its skin from chapping (keep in mind the fetus is floating around in amniotic fluid). The fetus is also covered with **lanugo**, a soft downy hair all over the body that helps the vernix stick to the skin. By the end of the second trimester, most organs are well developed. In fact, most of the human's billions of neurons are now in place. With brain development, there are additional changes—at this stage, the fetus will respond to the mother's voice and other loud noises.

A clever study conducted by Anthony DeCasper and his colleagues had 16 pregnant women read aloud a passage from the Dr. Seuss book *The Cat In the Hat* at regular intervals during pregnancy. When the babies were 2 to 3 days old, they were given a nipple attached to a sensing device. If they sucked more, they could hear their mother's voice reading one story; if they sucked less, they would hear her read a different story. The babies sucked whatever way it took to hear the familiar Dr. Seuss story, a clear indication that they remembered, and preferred, the familiar story. Similar studies have shown newborns recognize their mother's voice in utero, and also recognize songs heard repeatedly (such as the theme from a British soap opera, which was used in one study).

Finally, the last trimester is a time of "finishing up." Although most of the brain's neurons are in place, a great deal of brain growth continues at this time. Neurons will make connections with each other, and this final stage is an important time for **glial cells** to develop and give shape to the brain's major structures. Glial cells are sometimes called the glue of the brain because they hold neurons in place, but they also do much more than that. Glial cells insulate neurons, and provide oxygen and nutrients to neurons.

The last trimester is also the time when the fetus's lungs begin production of **surfactant**, a chemical needed to keep the air sacs in the lungs open; without surfactant the lungs collapse and the baby is unable to breathe. The ability to produce surfactant is linked to **the age of viability**, which is the earliest time when the fetus has the possibility of surviving if born. This is said to happen at around 24 weeks. However, at this very early age, the fetus will probably need a great deal of medical assistance, and is at high risk for long-term disability. Lung and brain maturity are the key determinants of survival and of future disability.

The greatest risk for babies born too early is **respiratory distress syndrome** (RDS), which happens when the baby's lungs do not produce enough surfactant to work on their own. In the early 1990s, doctors began to treat babies with synthetic surfactant, thereby significantly reducing the severity of RDS, and increasing the survival rates of preterm babies.

What Should Mom Be Doing?

Pregnant mothers often wonder what they can do to increase the likelihood of having a healthy pregnancy and a healthy baby. There is, of course, no short-age of advice from family, friends, books, the Internet, and even complete strangers. The advice expecting parents get can be confusing and contradictory. "Take it easy, you're pregnant" competes with "You need to exercise, you don't want to end up the size of a house." One well-meaning friend tells you to "Consume lots of dairy, calcium is important," and another warns, "Don't eat soft cheeses or deli meats, you may get a deadly bacterial infection." Other warnings include staying away from tuna, and fish in general because they have too much mercury. There is even advice about how to manage personal hygiene and beauty routines: "Don't dye your hair, get your nails done, get a suntan, sit in a hot tube, or shave your legs!" It's enough to make any rational woman crazy.

So what advice should an expectant mother heed and what can she or should she ignore? The only advice offered in this book is to talk to a doctor and to use common sense. You will often find that a doctor's advice confirms what your already know or what your instincts tell you. Imagine, for example, what a doctor might say about lifestyle and how closely this matches what most people now know at least in general terms. If a pregnant woman drinks a glass of wine, a beer or a cocktail, her unborn child takes the same drink. Whatever mother eats or drinks while pregnant goes through her bloodstream into the placenta and thus to the baby. The placenta does not filter out dangerous substances. If something is unhealthy for somebody who is not pregnant, such as smoking, inactivity, high fat foods, alcohol, drugs, and diseases, it is also unhealthy during pregnancy and unhealthy for the fetus. Additionally, anything the mother can become addicted to, including cigarettes or even caffeine, the developing fetus can become addicted to. And when the newborn infant is no longer receiving the addictive substances from the mother's bloodstream, that infant will suffer from the same withdrawal symptoms experienced by adults who quit smoking or drinking coffee "cold turkey." In their first days of life, they will be irritable and jittery and unnaturally flushed.

Both caffeine and cigarettes can be classified as **teratogens**, which are environmental substances that can damage the developing organism during pregnancy. A few general guidelines apply to teratogens. The first of these guidelines is that *more is worse.* For example, one cigarette during pregnancy is unlikely to have much of an effect; however, regular smoking places the fetus and the child it will become at significant risk of premature delivery, lower birth-weight, and higher rates of learning problems, antisocial behavior, and attention deficit disorder. Cigarette smoke contains more than 4,000 chemicals. Especially dangerous are nicotine and carbon monoxide, which work together to cut off the oxygen supply to the baby. The longer the oxygen is limited, the more damage occurs. So expectant mothers are encouraged to quit smoking as soon as possible.

A second rule about teratogens concerns *timing of exposure.* For many teratogens there appears to be a **critical period**—a time period when the organism is especially susceptible to influence. If a woman contracts German measles early in pregnancy, it can result in a range of serious consequences for her baby, including vision and hearing defects, heart defects, and mental retardation. Exposure during the last trimester is usually harmless. Timing can also affect which body part or system a given teratogen can potentially damage at different times during a pregnancy. For example, early in pregnancy the eyes, ears, and heart are developing and are therefore at greatest risk; later in the pregnancy these body parts are essentially done and therefore less susceptible to teratogenic effects. The most vulnerable system is the central nervous system, which continues to grow, develop, and change during the entire pregnancy.

A final general insight concerning teratogens is that *fetuses vary in vulnerability.* For example, two women consuming the same amount of alcohol can have different outcomes. One woman's child might be born with **fetal alcohol syndrome** (FAS), a pattern of lifelong mental and physical defects including distinct facial features, slowed growth, small head, and slowed intellectual and behavioral development. The other woman's child might have mild learning

Women who drink alcohol while they are pregnant may give birth to a newborn with fetal alcohol syndrome. The likelihood of this occurring depends on many variables, including how much alcohol is consumed and when during the pregnancy it is consumed. The most important thing to consider is that fetuses themselves vary in vulnerability. *(Shutterstock)*

and behavioral problems. When it comes to alcohol, nobody knows how much is "too much," and nobody knows which babies are most vulnerable. The safest behavior in this case is abstinence.

PRENATAL TESTING
In many parts of the world, and throughout history, parents knew little about what happens to the developing fetus. Was it a girl or boy? Was it healthy? Or in some instances, how many fetuses are there? Today's technological advances can give reasonably good answers to some of these questions. For example, **ultrasound technology** allows a technician to direct high-frequency sound waves at the womb; the echoes are then transformed into an image called a **sonogram**. This image gives a fairly clear picture of the fetus's structures, including its size, whether it is female or male, and in some instances, how many fetuses there are. It can also show where the embryo is implanted and the size of the placenta.

This non-invasive procedure appears to pose no risks to the fetus when used to monitor fetal growth, and can provide an early indication of some potential problems.

Other prenatal tests can provide different information. For example, if parents are concerned about genetic diseases or chromosomal abnormalities, there are a number of tests that can be run. **Genetic diseases** are illnesses carried by biological parents and passed down from one generation to the next. Sometimes the genes that produce such diseases are inherited by the child but related symptoms do not show up. In such cases, people may never know they are carriers unless the illness appears in their own offspring. It is possible, for example, for a child to be born with and manifest symptoms of sickle cell anemia (a dangerous blood disorder) even if the child's parents never had any symptoms. In contrast, **chromosomal abnormalities** are caused by damaged chromosomes or mutations in chromosomes. A common example of this is *Down's syndrome,* which is also called *trisomy-21* because instead of having two twenty-first chromosomes, the child affected with Down's syndrome has three. Physical characteristics related to this condition include a round face and flat nose, as well as assorted medical problems and cognitive disabilities.

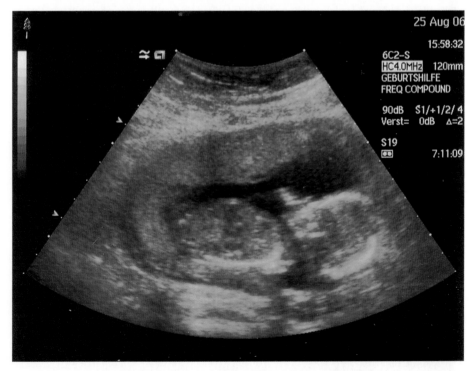

A sonogram of a human embryo at four months. *(Achim Raschka. Wikipedia)*

If a couple knows they or other family members have a genetic disease, if there is a family history of miscarriage or stillbirth, or if a couple is older, genetic counseling might be appropriate prior to conception to determine the potential for genetic or chromosomal problems. After conception, prenatal testing might be done to determine fetal risk. Around the middle of the third month, a procedure called **chorionic villi sampling** (CVS) can be done. A needle is used to remove a small piece of villi or hair-like extensions that attach the amniotic sac to the wall of the uterus. In about 10 days, preliminary results can tell the genetic make-up of the fetus Remember, the support structures, such as the placenta, amniotic sac, and villi all have the exact same genetic make-up as the fetus because the fetus and its support structures develop from one single zygote. There is approximately a 1 in 50 chance of miscarriage after CVS, so this procedure is not considered routine and is done only if there is a good reason.

Amniocentesis involves using ultrasound to guide the insertion of a needle through the woman's abdomen and uterus in order to remove a sample of amniotic fluid to test for chromosomal and genetic information. This procedure cannot be done until later in the pregnancy, about the fourth month. It takes about three weeks to get results. Like chorionic villi sampling, this procedure also carries a risk of miscarriage, but the risk is somewhat lower—about 1 in 150.

Before agreeing to any of these procedures parents should consider the post-test implications—in other words, what they will do with the information obtained. If a disorder were found, would an abortion be considered? Alternatively, would they want the information in order to prepare themselves to deal with a disabled child? Or would the information just cause more stress and anxiety during the pregnancy? Additionally, it is important to remember that although these procedures are fairly accurate, none is perfect. All of them can produce false positives, causing parents to worry unnecessarily (or in some cases abort unnecessarily), and false negatives, which means serious problems are accidentally missed. So, as with any medical procedure, the potential risks have to be weighed against potential benefits before deciding to go forward with testing.

BIRTH

The average pregnancy lasts 280 days from conception until delivery, but two weeks later or earlier than 280 days is considered normal. It is unclear what triggers the beginning of labor, but it seems the baby does something that triggers the mother's pituitary gland to release the hormone **oxytocin**, which in turn triggers uterine contractions. This is the first stage of birth. The uterus, a muscle, opens the cervix by pulling on it and then pushes the baby against the cervix to flatten it and force it open. When the involuntary contractions first begin, they are relatively short and spaced far apart. As labor progresses, the contractions come closer together and last increasingly longer. The cervix opening has to be about four inches in circumference for the baby to be delivered.

The second stage of birth occurs when the contractions push the baby into the birth canal, and then out into the world. Usually, the baby's head leads the way, facing downward. A shoulder is typically next, and then the baby turns itself around and the rest of the body emerges. The gentle hands of a birth attendant need only to guide and catch the newborn.

After delivery there is a lull in contractions. After a few minutes, the final stage of labor begins and more contractions expel the placenta and umbilical cord. A typical first birth takes about 16 to 17 hours, but this can vary tremendously and still be considered normal.

THE NEWBORN

For all newborns, those first seconds outside of the mother's body are a dramatic change from the prenatal environment. All of a sudden, the child must breath independently. In addition, the child no longer floats in warm cushioning amniotic fluid; instead, the weight of gravity presses down and its tiny body must manage the temperature of the environment, whether hot or cold. No longer are light and sound muffled by the womb; now the brain must process an abundance of new sensory information.

Healthy newborn babies also look a little unusual. Until they take their first few deep breaths, they can look blue or grayish. They also tend to be covered in vernix and even a little blood. Sometimes they look bruised and battered and have a pointy head. All of this is comes from being pushed through the tight birth canal.

In the first minutes after birth a valuable screening assessment can be done to get a general idea of the newborn's health. The test is named after the American doctor who developed it, Virginia Apgar, and it yields an **Apgar score.** The test is conducted one minute after birth and again 5 minutes after birth. It rates five characteristics 0, 1, or 2, and total scores can range from 0 (meaning immediate medical attention is needed) to 10 (everything looks great). The five characteristics can be remembered using the inventor's name as a mnemonic: **A**ppearance (skin color), **P**ulse (heart rate), **G**rimace (reflex response), **A**ctivity (muscle tone), and **R**espiratory effort.

PRETERM AND LOW BIRTH WEIGHT

The average pregnancy lasts 40 weeks from the first day of the last menstrual cycle; thus 40 weeks is considered full-term. The average size of a newborn is between 6 and 9 pounds. Babies born too early and/or too small are called

Medical Interventions During Delivery

Childbirth has always been a natural part of life, but death during childbirth has also been a natural part of life. Throughout history (and even today in some parts of the world) as many as one in four women die from complications during childbirth. Beginning in the late 1800s and increasing over the next hundred years, Western women began to give birth in hospitals, usually attended by a male doctor. Some scholars say this began the **medicalization of childbirth**—a term referring to the overuse of medical technologies during childbirth. By the late 1950s most women delivered in a hospital, strapped down, lying on their back, and under the influence of pain medication that left them semi-conscious. Then came the movement for **natural childbirth**, a movement characterized by educating expectant mothers and their partners about childbirth and giving them an active say in the decisions concerning their child's birth. Slowly, as women and families pushed for changes, hospitals and doctors adjusted.

Today, many medical procedures are available to make labor and delivery safer for mother and child. However, every medical procedure has risks, and the risks must be weighed against potential benefits. For example, approximately 70 percent of deliveries in the United States involve an **epidural**, medication injected into the spine to eliminate feeling from that point in the spine downward. The epidural alleviates the pain of contractions while allowing the mother to stay alert. Lessening or eliminating pain is certainly desirable during delivery, especially if labor is long. But an epidural also requires the mother to stay in bed for monitoring. This is problematic because labor goes faster when mothers are upright and use gravity and the weight of the baby to help open the cervix. Moreover, when mothers cannot feel contractions, they are not as good at pushing during delivery. With an epidural, labor and delivery are longer, and there is an increased risk of complications. In addition, medication crosses the

premature. In medical terms, birth before 38 weeks is **preterm.** An infant weighing less than 6 pounds is classified **low-birth-weight (LBW);** one weighing less than 3 ½ pounds is classified **very-low-birth-weight** (VLBW). Birth weight is the single best predictor of survival and health, and VLBW babies have an unusually high risk of death or long-term disability.

About 1 in 13 infants born in the United States is underweight. Some are born full term, and the condition is called **small-for-gestation**. Most underweight infants are born preterm. Causes of LBW are not always known, but research shows risk factors during pregnancy are poor prenatal care, inadequate placenta. Although there are no known long-term effects on the fetus, during their first days of life children born to mothers' who had an epidural have poorer reflexes and are more lethargic, making sucking and swallowing during feeding sluggish. This is particularly problematic when a mother is learning to breastfeed because it is extremely difficult to feed a weak and groggy baby.

When babies are unusually large or turned in the wrong direction, or if labor is prolonged, a surgical incision can be made through the mother's abdomen and uterus to remove the baby from the mother. This is called a **cesarean section** and saves the lives of many mothers and babies. Nonetheless, this surgery carries the same risks and increased recovery time associated with any major surgery. For newborns, being removed from the womb too early also poses risks. In some parts of the world more than one-third of all deliveries are by cesarean section, leaving one to wonder whether medical reasons or reasons of convenience are driving this trend.

Another sharply criticized medical procedure is the **induction of labor.** There are different ways to induce labor, or speed it along, such as puncturing the amniotic sac, giving hormones that get the cervix ready for delivery, or giving the hormone oxytocin to stimulate contractions. According to the CDC, in 2006, about one in five pregnant women in the United States had labor induced.

There are several criteria supporting the medical decision to induce labor: if the anticipated due date has passed, if the amniotic sac has ruptured, or if the mother has a medical condition that puts her health at risk. There are also convenience reasons for inducing labor, such as if a patient lives far from the hospital or a doctor will be on vacation. Problems can occur if the baby is delivered prematurely, and research findings indicate that labor induction should be practiced only when continuing the pregnancy presents a clear health risk to mother or child.

nutrition, stress, smoking, substance use, and multiple births (i.e. twins or triplets, etc.). Most LBW babies who receive care in a Neonatal Intensive Care Unit (NICU) will do well; nonetheless, later in life, they are at greater risk for attention, intellectual, and behavioral problems. Some, especially those without special care and those who are VLBW, will die. In a ranking of 31 industrialized countries, the United States ranked 30th on a international scale of infant mortality—one of the highest rates. The majority of the countries ranking above the United States (i.e., with lower infant mortality) provided free prenatal health care for all mothers.

At one time NICUs kept babies in temperature controlled incubators, and isolated them from family members due to fear of exposure to illnesses. These newborns were fed by a feeding tube, and were touched as little as possible to

Joey

Every parents' worst nightmare is to hear their newborn infant is not perfect. Lupe and Mike have relived that nightmare repeatedly. Their daughter Joey was born in the 26th week of Lupe's pregnancy, weighing only 1.5 pounds. Soon after her birth, Lupe and Mike were told Joey would probably die. Then they were told she would have brain damage, that she might be blind, that she might never walk. And after that, they were told she might never talk.

At first, Joey was too weak to nurse, so breast milk was dripped into her mouth. Cuddling with her was a challenge because she was almost always hooked up to tubes. There were countless treatments to deal with countless crises. Every step forward was countered with a setback—joy that Joey had gained a pound was followed by fear and anxiety when Joey had a seizure. In her first year Joey had surgery 14 times.

At 2 years old, Joey was diagnosed with Cerebral Palsy (CP) a condition resulting from brain damage that occurs during or just after birth. Today Joey has limited body control and knows only a handful of words. She cannot sit without support and does not reply to questions with words. But, this does not mean she is not capable: with a special harness that holds her upright, she is learning to walk, and although she does not respond to questions with words, she responds with smiles.

Lupe does not mind the stares and quick sympathetic glances from people whenever she takes Joey out in public, but they bother Mike. He also hates when people don't look. The family often encounters awkward moments when "normal" children ask their parents why Joey can't sit or talk, and the parents pretend to not hear the question.

The outlook for Joey is good. She has loving and involved parents, and she has access to good medical care. Advanced treatments and surgeries can minimize the effects of the CP, and new medications can control seizures. Joey also has many educational opportunities. Everyone who works with her recognize that Lupe and Mike are the experts on Joey.

It is still unknown if Joey will be able to graduate from a traditional high school, or even if she will ever be able to walk without supports. Perhaps she will be able to hold a job, support herself, and have a family, or perhaps she will need support throughout her adult life. The future is unknown. But given that she has exceeded all expectations so far, it seems fair to assume that she will continue to exceed the expectations of the "experts."

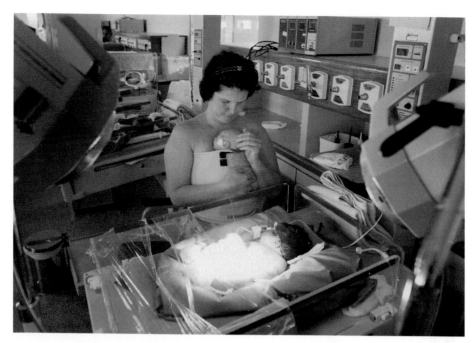

A mother using the kangaroo care method holds her baby against her skin. *(Antonio Scorza/AFP/Getty)*

avoid overstimulation. These techniques kept children alive but left families feeling somehow unworthy and detached. Some wonder whether such techniques also caused **sleeper-effects**, long-term consequences surfacing somewhat later in life, including higher rates of attention and learning difficulties.

Recent advances in high-tech interventions include techniques such as using synthetic surfactant to treat RDS, but most advances have been low-tech attempts to make the outside environment more "womblike." Interventions such as beds that mimic the sensation of floating in the amniotic sac (e.g., waterbed or hammock), bottle feeding a mother's breast milk even if the baby is too weak to nurse, and gentle massages have all enhanced the development of LBW babies. Benefits have also been found from **kangaroo care,** snuggling a baby against a parent's bare chest to maintain skin-to-skin contact and using the parent's body to keep the baby warm. This technique also allows the baby to hear a heartbeat just like it would if still in the womb.

CONCLUSION

Prenatal development begins with conception, followed by the germinal, embryonic, and fetal periods of pregnancy. Growth proceeds rapidly, and despite numerous risks, typically goes well. It is important for pregnant women to maintain good health and use common sense; eat well, stay active, eliminate

Revisiting Emmanuel and Seya

Earlier in this chapter we introduced a Tanzanian mother-to-be named Seya. An arduous lifestyle and a baby that died during delivery prompted a decision for the pregnant Seya to temporarily move to the home of her brother-in-law, who lived not far from a health center staffed by doctors and nurses.

After Seya went to live with Emmanuel's brother, Emmanuel and their daughters did not hear from her for two weeks. He and the girls worked hard to keep the house and fields going. Finally, Emmanuel's brother appeared to let them know Seya had given birth to a boy, and that both were healthy and resting.

Two weeks later Seya and her infant son returned home. She told Emmanuel that she had delivered the boy at the health center, but that no doctors or nurses were present, only a "traditional birth attendant." Seya said, "I know more about birth than the attendant. She kept me on my back. I'm lucky it was an easy birth—if there were problems that attendant would have let me die." Seya added that there was no running water, but that most things were clean.

After two months at home, Seya resumed working in the fields, but she still needed to feed her son often. She plans to stop breastfeeding in about a year, and hopes she can use birth control to prevent more pregnancies. Emmanuel wants more children and does not trust birth control. But he is willing to wait a few years before having another child.

stress, and avoid addictive substances. Childbirth involves three stages, contractions that widen and thin the cervix, pushing the baby through the birth canal, and delivering the placenta. Although sometimes overused, medical interventions during childbirth can save the lives of both mother and newborn. There are a number of risks associated with preterm birth and babies born too small, but low-tech interventions have proven remarkably successful.

Further Reading

Begley, Sharon, "How To Build A Baby's Brain." *Newsweek* (February 28, 1997). Accessed August 1, 2011; available from http://www.thedailybeast.com/newsweek/1997/02/28/how-to-build-a-baby-s-brain.html

"Does Breast-Feeding Reduce the Risk of Pediatric Overweight?" *Zero to Three* (September, 2007): 48-49; accessed August 1, 2011; available from http://main.zerotothree.org/site/DocServer/researchpractice10_07.pdf?docID=4321&JServSessionIdr009=gfkygctuo1.app2a

March of Dimes. Available at http://www.marchofdimes.com/

The United Nation's Children's Fund. Available at http://www.unicef.org/

CHAPTER 3

INFANT AND TODDLER DEVELOPMENT

BIRTH TO TWO YEARS

The first two years of life are an incredibly busy time for developing humans. At first, babies are completely dependent on caregivers, and unable to do much of anything. But within a two-year time span, most become walking-talking toddlers with their own opinions. For most babies, the journey involves growth and brain development and remarkable sensory, perceptual, and cognitive abilities.

These first two years are also a busy time for parents involved in the day-to-day care of an infant. Parents are filled with questions and concerns and can be overwhelmed by advice and suggestions offered by family members, friends, doctors and nurses, books, magazines, the Internet, and even well meaning strangers. Advice from these sources can be contradictory and sometimes goes against what feels right to parents. New parents feel like there are a million decisions to make, with no clear rules about what is best.

Developmental science shows that there is no one "right" way to raise a child. There are in fact many different routes to a healthy and happy childhood. This chapter describes some care requirements for humans at this stage of development—details related to feeding, sleeping, and immunizations. It also focuses on typical growth and brain development patterns as well as on the remarkable sensory, perceptual, and cognitive abilities babies develop during the first two years of life. The chapter concludes with a discussion of attachment theory, and how modern psychologists measure attachment.

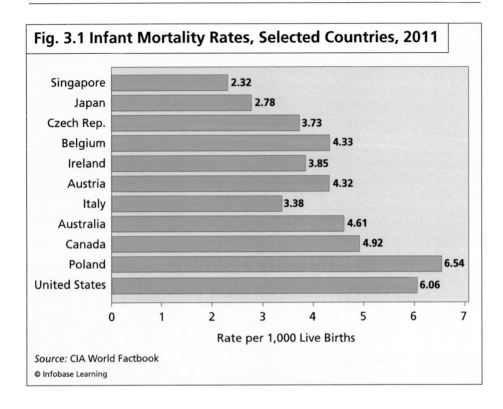

Fig. 3.1 Infant Mortality Rates, Selected Countries, 2011

Singapore 2.32
Japan 2.78
Czech Rep. 3.73
Belgium 4.33
Ireland 3.85
Austria 4.32
Italy 3.38
Australia 4.61
Canada 4.92
Poland 6.54
United States 6.06

Rate per 1,000 Live Births

Source: CIA World Factbook
© Infobase Learning

KEEPING BABY HEALTHY

Keeping infants and toddlers healthy is challenging. Globally, mortality rates indicate the first two years of life are among the riskiest in a lifetime. According to UNICEF, approximately 24,000 children die every day from preventable causes. Clean water, adequate nutrition, basic health care, and a basic education are needed to prevent these deaths.

What to Feed the Baby?

The saying "You are what you eat" is absolutely true for infants. The infant doubles its birth-weight by 5 months, and triples it by the first birthday. Adequate nutrition is vital to achieve expected growth. Breast milk from a well-nourished mother provides the exact ratio of protein, fat, and carbohydrates a growing baby needs. In fact, as the baby grows, the ratio of fat and protein in the mother's milk changes to meet changing needs. Even in a malnourished mother, breast milk can be sufficient for the first months of life. All international health organizations agree breastfeeding is the optimal method of feeding, especially in developing nations where formula can be costly for poor families and clean water may be scarce. But a mother's body only produces milk if the baby nurses.

Once mother stops nursing, milk production stops. So breastfeeding must begin right away.

Malnutrition is the leading cause of death during infancy. The most effective method of preventing malnutrition is breastfeeding. Yet, fewer than half of all infants are breastfed in the first six months of life. For a long time, formula makers aggressively marketed formula, leading mothers to see bottle feeding as more "modern." This happened in rich and poor nations alike. New mothers received free samples of formula, and once they stopped breastfeeding their milk production stopped. This was especially problematic in developing nations. If mothers could not afford formula after the free formula was used up, they watered down what they had. If they had no refrigeration, they used spoiled formula. If they lacked clean water, they used dirty bottles, mixing formula with contaminated water. International health agencies have struggled to counter decades of marketing by formula makers. Slowly, breastfeeding rates are increasing.

Most infant formulas adequately meet the nutritional needs of healthy babies, provided they are prepared as directed, under sanitary conditions. Formula is usually made from cow's milk or soymilk. These milk products are modified to match human baby needs. The protein content is reduced and the fat content is increased because human babies need milk with lots of fat (as opposed to cow babies that walk shortly after birth and thus need high protein milk). Invariably, human breast milk is far superior to formula for human babies. To begin with, it contains antibodies that lower an infant's chances of infection. Breastfed infants have lower rates of respiratory, gastrointestinal, and ear infections, lower rates of Sudden Infant Death Syndrome (SIDS), lower rates of colic, fewer allergies, and ultimately lower rates of mortality. In fact, recent evidence shows children who were breastfed as babies score higher on intelligence tests.

Breastfeeding is also better for mothers. Breastfeeding helps the uterus return to its original size quickly, it burns calories so mothers lose pregnancy weight, and it lowers the chances of breast and ovarian cancer. Finally, breastfeeding is cheap and convenient. There is no preparation, nothing to buy or wash, nothing to carry along when going out, and it will never run out as long as the mother continues to feed regularly (even when feeding twins or triplets).

One downside is that breastfeeding is a learned process and is not always easy. The first weeks can be difficult as both baby and mother learn what to do. Babies eat 6 to 8 times during the day and 1 to 2 times each night, so breastfeeding can be exhausting. Research in the United States shows a mother's decision to start and continue breastfeeding is largely determined by the support of those around her. When new mothers have others available to teach and support them, they are much more likely to begin and continue breastfeeding.

Fig. 3.2 Trends in the Percentage of Infants Under the Age of Six Months who are Exclusively Breastfed, 1995 and 2008

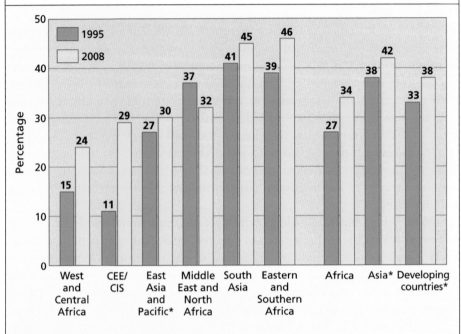

*Excluding China, due to lack of data.

Note: Analysis based on a subset of 86 countries with trend data, covering 84% of births in the developing world. Latin America and Caribbean were excluded due to insufficient data coverage. Regional trends indicate an increase from 26 to 46 percent, excluding Brazil and Mexico.

Source: UNICEF global databases 2010, from Multiple Indicator Cluster Services (MICS), Demographic Health Surveys (DHS) and other national surveys.

© Infobase Learning

Breastfeeding can also be difficult because only the mother can do it. This is problematic if the mother works, or if the father wants to participate. But there are solutions. Working mothers can collect milk with a breast pump, or the baby can be fed formula when the mother is at work. Fathers can get involved by rocking, changing, or feeding the baby with bottles of breast milk or formula.

Some mothers cannot breastfeed (for example, adoptive and foster mothers) or should not breastfeed (for example, mothers with an illness like HIV that can be passed on to the baby and mothers using drugs to treat an illness or street-drugs). For these mothers, formulas work well.

Where, How Long, and How Should Baby Sleep?

Sleep is a tremendous concern for new parents. How much should the baby sleep? Where should it sleep? Should it be "trained to sleep?" For some of these questions, science gives clear answers. For example, most newborns sleep 16 hours a day, in roughly 3 to 4 hour cycles of sleep and wake. Gradually daytime sleep diminishes and by their third birthday children sleep about 12 hours a day, with only 1 hour during daytime. For other questions, cultural practices and parental comfort guide decision making. One issue often debated is co-sleeping. Some believe parents and baby sleeping in the same bed is natural, whereas others consider this to be obscene or dangerous. In most parts of the world co-sleeping has always been and continues to be the norm. But in cultures where families have multiple bedrooms, co-sleeping is less common. Co-sleeping also takes many forms. In Japan, parents and baby share a mat or futon. In the Philippines, Vietnam, and Latin America parents sleep with baby in a hammock next to the bed or in a basket in bed between parents.

The American Academy of Pediatrics (AAP) advises against co-sleeping, citing concerns about adults rolling onto babies or suffocation from soft bedding. The AAP additionally cites concerns about children being placed at risk for SIDS. Supporters counter that co-sleeping is safe when proper bedding is used, such as a firm mattress, and as long as parents are not under the influence of drugs or alcohol. Additionally, sleeping close to baby makes nighttime feedings easier and makes breastfeeding more likely. Mother and baby have synchronized sleep cycles, meaning baby spends more time asleep at night and require shorter night-time feedings. Cultures that routinely practice co-sleeping, such as Hong Kong, have lower rates of SIDS. There are scientific arguments on both sides of this issue, and common sense and what feels right for parents is probably the best guide.

Immunizations

Illnesses such as whooping cough, polio, measles, and tetanus were once common killers of children. Today, because of immunizations, these illnesses rarely kill children who live in developed nations. *Immunization* (or *vaccine*) is a small dose of inactive virus administered by injection, inhalation, swallowing, or wearing a patch. This inactive virus stimulates the body's natural disease-fighting system, the immune system. If the body later encounters an active virus, the immune systems can prevent the illness. In developed nations rates of immunizations for some illnesses can be as high as 92 percent. Millions of children, however, particularly those in the poorest parts of the world, remain at risk for contracting diseases that can be prevented by immunizations.

Given what we know about the power of immunization, it is somewhat surprising that some parents living in developed nations do not have their children immunized. Some argue the illnesses are so uncommon it is unlikely their child will contract them (ironically the reason these illnesses are rare is that immunizations have worked). This argument is dangerous because immunizations protect not only the immunized child but also protects others who are too

Back to Sleep

Sudden infant death syndrome (SIDS) occurs when a seemingly healthy infant stops breathing while asleep and dies. For SIDS to be diagnosed, an infant must be between 2 and 12 months of age, and there must be no other medical explanation for the death. Developmentalists discovered that rates of SIDS vary across cultures. Examining childrearing practices, they found that in cultures with lower rates of SIDS, infants were more likely to be breastfed, sleep in close proximity to others, and sleep on their backs. This prompted more research, with a particular focus on infants who died from SIDS. The findings showed that children who died from SIDS were more likely to have a mother who smoked during pregnancy and lived in a household with a smoker. Infants who died from SIDS were also more likely to be male, have a low birth weight, be warmly dressed, formula fed, and the offspring of a teen parent. It is important to note that all of these factors are not absolute determinants for SIDS: Many children who die from SIDS have no risk factors, and many children with all the risk factors do not die from SIDS. However, when little is known about a condition a basic understanding of correlates is useful.

In 1992, a campaign to combat SIDS was initiated. Called the "Back-to-Sleep" campaign, it was led by doctors who encouraged parents to put infants to sleep on their backs rather than on their stomachs. This ran counter to many Western ideas about sleep, including the widespread belief that babies sleeping on their back would be more prone to choking on spit-up. Nonetheless, advertisements in magazines, posters and pamphlets in doctors' offices, and encouragement from medical personnel persisted, and between 1992 and 2006 the number of back-sleeping babies in the United States increased from 13 percent to 76 percent, and SIDS rates went from 1.2 per 1,000 to .55 per 1,000. Supporters of the campaign argue that the back to sleep campaign was a success.

young or too sick to be immunized (such as fetuses in the womb and cancer or HIV patients). Others refuse immunizations because of concerns about potential side-effects; however, most potential side-effects are rare, and when they do occur, they tend to be less dangerous than the actual illness—the most common side-effects are soreness at injection site or a temporary fever.

In the mid-1990s the number of children diagnosed with autism increased dramatically in the United States, leading some to argue that the increase was the direct result of the MMR (Measles-Mumps-Rubellea) vaccine. One could argue that this assumption made sense on some level because the MMR vaccine is administered shortly after the first birthday, about the same time autism symptoms first appear. Numerous well-controlled studies have debunked this myth, however, showing that rates of autism are the same in immunized and non-immunized children. Nonetheless it remains a popular argument against immunizations.

At about the same time, a similar problem was occurring in Tanzania (home of the Makanza family introduced in Chapter 2). A leading cause of death in Tanzania is tetanus, a disease that can easily be prevented by vaccination. But in the 1990s, vaccination rates dropped, largely because of unfounded rumors about the tetanus vaccine. These rumors began at a Catholic mission hospital where a doctor was concerned the vaccine was laced with a hormone used in birth control. Even though the vaccine was tested and proven pure, the rumor spread and many women were not vaccinated and were thus put at risk.

BODY GROWTH AND DEVELOPMENT

New parents are often shocked at how quickly babies grow. Approximately half of all growth happens in the first two years of life, so doubling the 2-year-old child's height is a fairly accurate prediction of adult height. Motor skills and cognitive abilities also change dramatically during these first two years. A newborn cannot hold its head up and communicates by crying; two years later she will run, use a spoon, and say, "more cookies." These are remarkable changes in so short a time! They are due to bone and muscle growth, as well as to dramatic changes in the nervous system.

There are two general principles about growth. One is the *cephalocaudal principle*. This is the idea that growth occurs from the head downward (in Greek *cephalo* is head and *caudal* is tail). This pattern is exemplified by the infant's gross motor skills development. *Gross motor skills* involve large body movements (*gross* in this context means *big*). The first thing a baby can do is hold its head up; the next is to use the arms to push the torso up. Soon it can roll over. Next the infant will hold its torso steady and sit up without support. Later it will crawl, then stand while holding onto something, and finally walk. This body control proceeds from head down.

Simultaneously, growth proceeds outward from the spine. This is called the *proximodistal* principle. Growth emanates from the proximal (near) to the distal (far). Fine motor skill development exemplifies this principle. *Fine motor skills* are abilities that involve small body movements, particularly movement of the hands and fingers (*fine* in this context means *small*). First a baby stares at and bats at an object; at around 3 months it will purposely swipe its arms at a nearby object. Between 4 and 6 months of age, it will reach and grasp objects using all fingers against the palm, and after the first birthday, it will use the pincer grasp (thumb against forefingers) to pick up and hold small things. Arm and hand control proceeds from spine outward.

These two principles also exemplify growth in the nervous system. First the head, then the trunk, and then extremities grow (cephalocaudal), and the first part of the nervous system to develop is the neural tube, which later becomes the brain and spinal cord. Later, nerves close to the spinal cord grow; ultimately nerves further from the spinal cord grow (proximodistal).

The Nervous System

The nervous system is made up of the brain and spinal cord (the central nervous system) and all of the neural tissue throughout the body (the peripheral nervous system). The basic unit of the nervous system is the neuron. The neuron sends messages: While these messages are inside the neuron they are electrical; when they are between neurons, they are chemical.

Neurons come in many shapes and sizes, but all have a cell body, axons, and dendrites. Long **axons** carry electrical signals through the neuron and send the message to other neurons. Bushy **dendrites** shoot off the cell body and pick up messages from other neurons. But axons and dendrites do not touch; a gap called the **synapse** connects the axon of one neuron with a dendrite of another neuron.

Neurotransmitters are the chemical means of communication between neurons. They are chemicals released by the axon and picked up by the dendrite. Many axons are covered with myelin. **Myelin** is a fatty substance wrapped around the axon to protect it and help messages travel quickly.

A baby's brain has about 100 billion neurons, and each neuron might have thousands of axons and dendrites that form thousands of synaptic connections with other neurons. Messages traveling through the brain are electrical impulses while inside the neuron, and are sped along through the axon by fatty sheaths of myelin. In the synaptic gaps, transmission of the signal is through chemicals called neurotransmitters. So a message traveling from neuron to neuron through the nervous system alternates between being electrical and chemical. It is a simple process in an amazingly complex organ.

Brain Development

A great deal of brain development happens prior to birth, and by the time the baby is born the brain is proportionately the largest part of the body. At birth the brain weighs about 25 percent of its adult weight. Compared to the rest of the newborn's body, the brain is very heavy (the average newborn weighs about 7 ½ pounds, which is about 5 percent of adult size). At age 2, the brain weighs about 75 percent of its adult weight, and by age 5 it weighs about 90 percent of its adult weight. What accounts for this tremendous increase in weight? Certainly not new neurons because neurons are not made after birth. The increase is primarily due to myelination of neurons and synaptic growth in different areas of the brain.

Asynchrony in Brain Development

At different times, different regions of the brain experience growth spurts in synaptic connections. For example, immediately after birth, the axons and

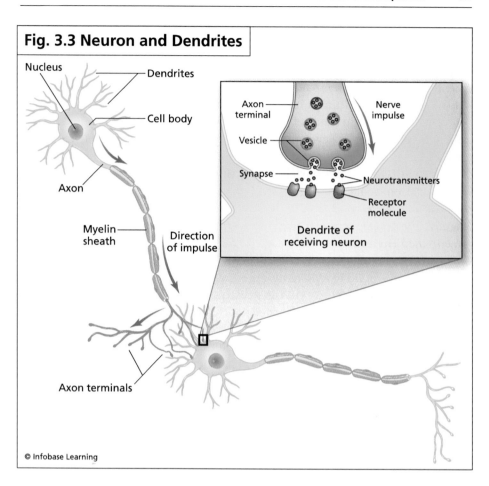

Fig. 3.3 Neuron and Dendrites

Nucleus

Dendrites

Cell body

Axon

Myelin sheath

Direction of impulse

Axon terminals

Axon terminal

Nerve impulse

Vesicle

Synapse

Neurotransmitters

Receptor molecule

Dendrite of receiving neuron

© Infobase Learning

dendrites in the visual cortex will grow and make countless synaptic connections—way more than will ever be needed. This is called **overproduction**. Then, over the next few years, growth in synaptic connections slows down and unused synapses are **pruned** off and lost. So by age 5, the visual cortex is essentially complete. Similarly, during the first year of life there is a growth spurt in the motor cortex, the brain region responsible for moving the body. This growth spurt lasts several years, which explains why a newborn baby is not able to lift its own head but can walk and run by age 2. These growth spurts in different regions of the brain continue all the way through adolescence and into early adulthood.

Research on Brain Development

So judging by brain weight, most brain development happens very early in life, leaving some to argue the first two years of brain development are the most important. However, using brain weight to gage growth is a crude index, one that does not take into account a host of other features. One obvious difficulty in determining how a brain develops is direct access to developing brains. Until recently, most of what was known about brain development came from animal studies or from examining a human brain during an autopsy. There are many problems with both methods of investigation. For one thing, the brains of other animal species may not develop the same way that a human brain develops. For another, the brain of a deceased baby cannot show how the brain works.

Even with their limitations, however, animal studies have been a rich source of information about brain growth. For example, in the early 1960s studies on adult rats were conducted by psychologist Mark Rosenzweig and his colleagues. The researchers placed rats in enriched and deprived environments. An enriched environment was a cage with a water bottle, a food source, a running wheel, toys and other rats. The deprived environment was smaller and had no running wheel, no toys, and no other rats. When rats from the two groups were compared in this study (and in subsequent studies), it was found that rats from enriched environments learned to run mazes more quickly than rats from deprived environments. Moreover, autopsy showed that their brains were heavier and exhibited more folds (an indicator of more extensive brain growth).

Human research has supported the findings of this research with rats. In the late 1990s brain researcher Charles Nelson discovered that large numbers of children in Romania were in state-run orphanages that provided basic needs (such as food and shelter) but provided virtually no social, emotional, or physical stimulation. Compared to other children these orphans smiled and laughed less, had poorer language skills, exhibited lower intelligence and higher rates of mental illness, and showed less brain activity. In 2001 Nelson and his colleagues began *The Bucharest Early Intervention Project,* a project designed to remove children from these orphanages and place them in foster families. They began by recruiting and training as many foster parents as possible. Children between 6 months and 2½ years were placed with families. The researchers continue to follow the development of the children with foster families as well as children of the same age still living in the orphanages. Those with foster families have made greater gains in language, intelligence, social skills, and most aspects of mental health.

In another series of groundbreaking studies, David Hubel and Torsten Wiesel studied the brains of kittens. In some of the studies they anesthetized the kittens and inserted microelectrodes into their brains to see which brain cells were working when the animals looked at different images. In other studies they examined kittens with one eye stitched closed for different lengths of time. They found that a cat's visual system is wired to work at birth but will atrophy or waste away if not used. Cats that did not use their eyes lost the neural connections in the visual cortex. Hubel and Wiesel concluded that cats had to use their eyes in order for the brain cells in their visual cortex to maintain the connections that were present at birth. This was science's first clear evidence of neural plasticity; because of their research, Hubel and Wiesel won the 1982 Nobel prize awarded for work in physiology or medicine.

Neural plasticity is the term used to explain that neural connections can be altered through experience. Plasticity refers to flexibility, and the main idea behind this concept is that the brain works in accordance with the "use-it or lose-it" principle. Neural connections and pathways used over and over are strengthened, but connections and pathways never or seldom used atrophy and are lost. For example, the brain at birth is wired to hear every phonemic sound in every human language. If children hear sounds from only one language, the pathways for the phonemes in that language are strengthened, but pathways for other phonemic sounds are lost. So an adult who was raised hearing only English will have difficulty hearing phonemes unique to Japanese or Russian because those neural connections were never stimulated and were lost. Moreover, that adult will hear a second language through the filter of his or her first language. This is why most adults who learn a second language speak it with an accent.

Recent advances in medical technology have given scientists better ways to examine the adult brain at work, but most of these procedures do not work well with infants because they require complete stillness (not practical with an infant) or injections of radioactive particles (not usually advised without a medical need). However, this field of inquiry changes quickly, and every day less invasive and more accurate devices are being developed for infant brain imaging.

Sensitive Periods

Animal studies have confirmed that very extreme sensory deprivation can result in permanent loss of functioning and perhaps brain damage. Additionally, there are certain time periods that sensory stimulation appears to be especially important. A **critical period** is a short time span during which to acquire a new skill, but only if the person that is to learn this skill is exposed to some trigger in the environment. Hubel and Wiesel found that young kittens with one eye stitched closed and deprived of light for too long could not see once the eye was opened and permitted stimulation. Similarly, in some species of birds, such as finches and canaries, there is a brief time period during which a young bird must listen to the song of an older bird. If the bird never hears the song or hears it after the critical time period, the young bird will never learn the song.

Because scientists are unsure of when exact time periods occur or whether or not it is possible to acquire a skill past the "critical period," they often use the term **sensitive period** when studying this phenomenon in humans. A sensitive period is a broader and less specific time period that is optimal for some

Baby Mozart, Baby Bach, Baby Einstein—Baby Overload

In the early 1990s Frances Rauscher and Gordon Shaw studied 36 college students who participated in three 10-minute situational exercises; they listened to Mozart, they listened to a relaxation tape, and they sat in silence. After each segment of the exercise they took an IQ test. After listening to Mozart, the students scored a little higher in one subsection of the IQ test, but this increase was temporary.

Clearly there were problems with this study. To begin with, 36 college students is too small a sample to yield any significant data, and administering the same IQ test over and over is not good science. Moreover, scientists conducting similar subsequent studies did not get the same results.

This research was never done with children as participants. Nonetheless, the "Mozart Effect" indicated by the first study took off. In Georgia, babies were given a free Mozart CD, and Florida passed a law requiring state-funded childcare centers to play classical music. An industry was born.

Even today, commercials tout "Your baby can have a bigger brain, but only if you purchase this product." Well-intentioned parents train their babies with flashcards, sit children in front of "educational" shows, play classical music during naptime, and purchase battery operated toys with flashing lights and nonstop tinkling electronic music. Electronic gadgets are sold to teach babies colors, shapes, numbers, letters, and sign language. Parent testimonials in commercials

ability to emerge as a result of something that happens in the environment. It is still possible for development to occur later; it is just more difficult to bring on. For example, some infants are born with cataracts in their eyes; if they are left untreated, the neural pathways in the visual cortex atrophy and die. But if the infants have corrective surgery within the first few months of life, their eye(s) will experience normal visual stimulation, and the neural pathways in the visual cortex will be strengthened. Early surgery has a high success rate, but later surgery—after the growth spurt in the visual cortex—has lower rates of success. Surgery in adulthood has no success whatsoever. The visual stimulation is too late—the brain is no longer open to changes in the visual cortex.

Evidence suggests there are also sensitive periods for language, social, and emotional development in humans. For example, Nelson found that the Romanian orphans placed with foster families prior to their second birthday made significant gains in language. However, orphans placed after their second birthday failed to make significant gains. Both sets of children had experienced early deprivation and then a rich language environment, but it appears the that advertise these products rave, "I plopped him in front of the television and he couldn't take his eyes off it" or "She was entertained for hours and I could go about my business" or "It keeps him mesmerized." Worldwide, more than 2 billion dollars a year are spent on "educational" products for children under the age of three.

Is there evidence these products work? No. In fact, some studies have found negative effects. For this reason, the American Academy of Pediatrics warns against any television or videos for children under age 2. The AAP notes that there is little research supporting "educational" television for infants, citing instead strong research showing the benefits of adult-child interactions, such as talking, singing, and playing.

Advertisements for "educational" products often imply some company's product is better than a parent's lullaby or story. One commercial shows a girl alone in her bed flipping the pages of a book and listening to a recording of her mother's voice reading the story; the mother is downstairs sitting in front of a television set. It is impossible to imagine how being alone listening to a recording is better than cuddling and interacting as a parent reads aloud, and yet this is what the commercial implies!

An understimulating environment can certainly damage children (remember the rats), but it is also important for parents not go too far to the other extreme. Normal everyday interactions are what children need. If you think about it, Mozart, Bach, and Einstein all managed to do well without "educational" products.

sensitive period for language development occurs in the first two years of life. If the rich language environment is provided too late, the window for significant gains has closed.

Wrapping up the Brain

Brain research has shown that children should grow up in "rich" environments; those who do will have larger and more complex brains. Additionally, there appear to be sensitive periods during which brain development and acquisition of certain abilities intersect, so deprivation during certain times can result in permanent brain damage. Fortunately, research indicates a "rich" environment does not mean surrounding a baby with fancy gadgets, and extreme deprivation is unlikely to occur under normal circumstances. For children, human interaction is the most stimulating activity. Listening to mother sing, gazing into father's eyes while being rocked, playing paddy-cake with a sibling, or sitting on a babysitter's lap as she reads are all examples of activities that stimulate the brain.

SENSORY AND PERCEPTUAL SKILLS

We can't very well ask infants "Can you smell this, or see or hear or taste that?" But developmentalists have designed some very clever experiments, which show that newborns' senses are fairly well prepared at birth. As DeCasper illustrated with *The Cat in The Hat* study, babies can hear even prior to birth. They can also distinguish different tastes. In a series of experiments, Jacob Steiner and his colleagues observed the facial expressions of newborns immediately before and after they were exposed to various tastes and smells, thereby determining not only whether they could sense something, but also how much something had to change before the difference was noticed.

Although infants can see as soon as they are born, they are nearsighted at first and can focus best at 8 to 10 inches (the distance a parent's face would be during feedings). They are also capable of seeing various colors and can track a moving object. Over the first two years their vision improves, and by age 2, their ability to see details from a distance matches an adult's.

Perceptual skills refer to how an individual interprets, or makes sense of, sensory information. Again, researchers have conducted some clever research. One method of inquiry was to present infants with two stimuli and observe which drew more attention. This is how researchers learned infants prefer bright colors and sharp contrasts.

Another method for studying infant perception is to present the same stimuli over and over. When a new stimulus is presented, most infants first show an increase in attention (eyes open wider, movements change, heart-rate changes); after repeated exposure, they get used to the stimulus and stop responding to it. This decline in response to things that become familiar is called **habituation**. Researchers can also see if infants know the difference between old stimuli and new stimuli. **Dishabituation** occurs if after habituation something new is presented, and there is an increase in response again. This method is how researchers learned the infant can tell the difference between tastes such as sweet and sour or tell the difference between phonetic sounds such as /pa/ and /ba/. In one study, they repeated the sound /pa/ over and over at regular intervals until the infant habituated and showed no response. They then used /ba/ in place of a /pa/. If the infant dishabituated and became alert again, it was clear that the difference was noticed.

Another perceptual skill studied extensively is **depth perception**. Eleanor Gibson and Richard Walk (1960) created a clever piece of equipment called a "visual cliff"—a rectangular table with a hard transparent surface. Below the surface is a checkerboard cloth. On one side of the table the cloth is directly under the transparent surface. This is the shallow end. At the table's midpoint there is a drop of several feet and the cloth is far below the transparent surface for the other half of the table (the deep end). Gibson and Walk placed 6-month-olds who were able to crawl at the shallow end of the table and had a parent stand

and call them from the deep end. Most children began to crawl but stopped and would not crawl past the "cliff." From this behavior, the researchers deduced that infants perceive depth. Non-crawling younger children and crawling older children were also held over the shallow end and then the deep end while their heart-rates were monitored. Both groups showed a change in heart rate, indicating they noticed a difference. But heart rates for non-crawlers decreased, indicating curiosity, whereas heart rates for crawlers increased, indicating fear. From this, researchers were able to conclude that depth perception is present at an early age, but only experience teaches infants to fear a sudden drop.

COGNITIVE DEVELOPMENT

The physical, sensory, and perceptual development of a child is closely linked to cognitive development. There are several theoretical approaches to looking at cognitive development. Piaget, for instance, proposed four stages of cognitive development; at each stage, humans understand the world in a qualitatively different way.

Piaget's Sensorimotor Stage

According to Piaget, between birth and 2 years of age, children are in the *sensorimotor* stage. At this stage children begin to use symbols such as language, and infants use their senses and motor skills to understand the world. So if a child is presented with a rattle, it might learn about it by staring, sucking, or grabbing. As motor skills develop, ways of interacting with objects change.

One of the most important milestones during this stage is *object permanence*, the understanding that things continue to exist even when they cannot be sensed. Piaget noted this skill develops slowly. When a brightly colored toy is waved in front of an interested 2-month-old and then placed behind a screen, the baby will show surprise when the screen is quickly moved away and the toy is not there but will not actively search for it. By 6 to 8 months of age, babies will search for lost objects, such as a toy that falls from the crib or food that falls from the highchair; some will even make a game of drop and search. But if the object is completely out of view, the game ends and the search stops. By 12 months, however, infants persist—they now have basic object permanence.

Some methods Piaget used to study object permanence, such as covering a toy with a blanket, have been criticized because they require the infant to grab and pull the blanket off the toy. The fine motor skills required to do this develop over the first year, so it is impossible to know if failure to grab and pull the blanket is due to cognitive or motor skills. More recent research that removed this motor component indicates that children may have object permanence at an even younger age than Piaget proposed. Additionally, research has shown that object permanence appears to be linked to changes in the frontal lobe of the brain.

SOCIAL AND EMOTIONAL DEVELOPMENT

During the first years of life infants are completely dependent on caregivers for their survival. But their social world quickly changes, and by the end of this stage, toddlers can walk, talk, and show discriminating responses to social situations.

Attachment Theory

Infants with a regular caregiver show an obvious preference for that caregiver over a stranger and show contentment when the caregiver is around. Between 6 and 24 months many infants show **stranger anxiety** by clinging to caregiver when a stranger is present; they also show **separation anxiety** by crying or protesting when separated from the caregiver. These behaviors, which emerge at about the same time that object permanence emerges, peak during the end of the first year of life and diminish over the next year.

Attachment is an enduring emotional bond to another person. There are different theoretical approaches about why this bond initially forms. For the learning theorists of the early to mid-20th century, the bond formed because infants need food, and this need is most often satisfied by a parent. Therefore, the parent becomes associated with feeding, and ultimately becomes a reinforcer. In other words, the infant becomes attached to the parent because it associates the parent with food.

In the late 1950s, however, Harry Harlow and his associates proposed a contrasting theory of attachment. Harlow and his team conducted a series of studies on orphaned infant monkeys. Each monkey had two wire "mothers" placed in its cage—one was wire mesh and the other was covered with terrycloth. Half the monkeys were fed from a bottle affixed to the wire mother, and the other half were fed from a bottle affixed to the terrycloth mother. All of the monkeys spent at least 165 days with their "mothers," and regardless of where feeding took place, when given the choice, all monkeys spent more time with the terrycloth mother. When a frightening object, such as a mechanical toy robot, was placed in their cages, the monkeys ran to the terrycloth monkey. Even after a year of separation, the monkeys ran to the terrycloth mother and clung to her. In contrast, monkeys raised with monkey mothers showed little interest in either the terrycloth or wire mothers. If the learning theorists had been correct, the monkeys should have become attached to the "mother" they were fed by. Because this was clearly not the case, Harlow concluded that "contact comfort" is more important than feeding. These findings spurred new theories of attachment.

Ethology is the scientific study of animal behavior, especially as it occurs in natural environments. Ethological theorists propose that because infants need adults to survive, attachments keep mother and child in close proximity, thereby increasing the chances the infant will survive. The infant has an innate ability to

Harry F. Harlow with the terrycloth and wire mesh monkey mothers. *(Photo by Nina Leen/Time Life Pictures/Getty)*

signal the caregiver, and caregivers are biologically predisposed to react to these signals. For example, when infants have a need, they reflexively cry. Adults are biologically wired to respond to that cry, so they come to the aid of the infant. In fact, various studies have found physiological changes in adults hearing a crying infant, including changes in blood pressure, skin conductance, and heart rate (e.g., Brewster, Nelson, McCanne, Lucas, & Milner, 1998; Frodi & Lamb, 1978).

British attachment theorist **John Bowlby** adopted an ethological perspective. But he also believed the mother-infant attachment bond that was critical in the psychoanalytic perspective was important for later social development. He proposed infants form an internal model of attachment, and this internal model influences how they react in attachment relationships later in life, such as with romantic partners.

Mary Ainsworth had similar ideas about attachment. However, she wanted to develop a way to distinguish between different types of attachment relationships. She believed some caregiver-child relationships were secure and others insecure. She developed **The Strange Situation**, a standardized laboratory procedure conducted with toddlers between 12 and 18 months. A **standardized** procedure is always done the same way and has clear and consistent scoring. Ainsworth wanted to gradually increase infants' stress and then observe how the infants reacted to their mothers. She did not observe the mothers' behaviors, because if they knew they were being watched they might behave differently than they would normally behave in this situation. She conceptualized the situation as being similar to that experienced in a waiting room at a doctor's office. The procedure takes place in 8 episodes each lasting 3 minutes. (See Table 3.1).

Based on observations of children in these episodes, especially episodes 5 and 8, Ainsworth classified children as *secure* if they readily separated from mother, were able to explore the environment, sought comfort when distressed, and were consoled by the mother; she classified as *insecure avoidant* those children who avoided contact with mother, especially when distressed, and showed no preference for mother over stranger; and as *insecure ambivalent* those children who showed little exploration, were overly upset at separations, were not soothed by mother's return, and alternated between wanting to be comforted and resisting contact.

Ainsworth argued that the first year of mother-infant interactions influences attachment classification. Numerous studies have found that mothers who respond appropriately to their infants' needs and are emotionally available, have securely attached relationships. Mothers who are not responsive and reject their infants have insecure avoidant attachments, and mothers who show inconsistent or unpredictable caregiving have insecure ambivalent attachments.

The Strange Situation procedure has been used extensively, and most evidence suggests there are both short-term and long-term consequences to attachment classification. Securely attached infants grow up to be more social, more

TABLE 3.1
The Strange Situation

Episode	What happens
1	Researcher brings mother and infant to a room with two chairs and a pile of toys on the floor. Room is equipped with one-way mirror or camera so researchers can observe.
2	Mother and infant are alone in room.
3	A stranger enters the room and sits for 1 minute. Talks to mother for 1 minute, and finally gets on floor to engage infant with toys for 1 minute.
4	Mother stands up and leaves stranger and infant alone.
5	Mother returns and stranger leaves so mother and infant are alone.
6	Mother leaves so infant is alone.
7	Stranger returns and if necessary attempts to soothe the infant.
8	Mother returns and stranger leaves so mother and infant are alone again.

independent, less aggressive, more empathetic, and more emotionally mature when they are in early and middle childhood. As adolescents they are more likely to be rated as leaders and have higher self-esteem. They are less likely to become sexually active early, and they get better grades.

The procedure has also been used in many different cultures. Generally research findings support Ainsworth's basic premises; however, some scientists express concern that infants in different cultures might all experience different levels of stress from being left alone.

And finally, most of Ainsworth's research was done on mothers, so the term "mother" was used when discussing her work. Ainsworth's methods have also been used with other attachment figures such as fathers, babysitters, and siblings. Additionally, attachment classifications can change over time depending on the consistency of the quality of parenting; moreover, a child might exhibit a secure attachment with one parent and an insecure attachment with another parent.

CONCLUSION

This first two years of life are a remarkable time of rapid growth and development. It takes tremendous effort on the part of parents, and the communities that support parents, to keep children healthy. Babies come into the world with fairly mature sensory and perceptual systems, and even their cognitive abilities mature rapidly. Sensitive caregivers who provide support and encourage exploration ultimately lay the foundation of healthy social and emotional development.

Further Reading

Belkin, Lisa. "Child Care Costs More Than College." *The New York Times* (August 9, 2010). Accessed August 1, 2011; available from http://parenting.blogs.nytimes.com/2010/08/09/child-care-costs-more-than-college/?scp=10&sq=Daycare&st=cse

Brewster, A., J.P. Nelson, T.R. McCanne, D.R. Lucas, and J.S. Milner. "Gender Differences in Physiological Reactivity to Infant Cries and Smiles in Military Families." *Child Abuse and Neglect* 22, no. 8 (1998): 775–778.

Frodi, A.M., and M.E. Lamb. "Sex Differences in Responsiveness to Infants: A Developmental Study of Psychophysiological and Behavioral Responses. *Child Development* 49 (1978): 1182–1188.

La Leche League International. Available at http://www.lalecheleague.org/

National Infant and Toddler Child Care Initiative. Available at http://nitcci.nccic.acf.hhs.gov/

Steiner, J.E. Human Facial Expressions in Response to Taste and Smell Stimulation. In. H.W. Reese and L.P. Lipsitt (Eds.) *Advances in Child Development and Behavior, Vol. 13* (pp. 257–296). New York: Academic Press, 1979.

Nelson, C. The Bucharest Early Intervention Project. Available at www.childrenshospital.org/cfapps/research/data_admin/Site2204/mainpageS2204P0.html

Zero to Three. Available at http://www.zerotothree.org/

Zeskind. P.S., J. Sale, L.A. Maio, L. Huntington, and J.R. Weiseman. (1985). "Adult Perceptions of Pain and Hunger Cries: A Synchrony of Arousal." *Child Development* 56 (1985): 549–554.

CHAPTER 4

DEVELOPMENT
IN EARLY CHILDHOOD

AGE TWO TO AGE FIVE

Early childhood, characterized by almost constant movement, chatter, and experimentation, is one of the most fun age groups to observe. Some call this stage of a child's development the "preschool" years, but others worry that "pre-" implies children are not learning and prefer to call this time the "play" years. No matter what it is called, the changes that take place at this time are dramatic. At 2 years of age the child still looks and acts like a toddler, with a disproportionately large head, short arms and legs, and big belly. Two-year-olds are unstable when running and jumping, and are willing to play with whatever or whoever is nearby. By the end of the fifth year, the child is taller, leaner, has preferred toys and friends, and looks and acts like a kid.

This chapter begins with a description of the physical growth that occurs during early childhood and the rapidly changing abilities in large and small body movements. We then describe changes in the brain and explore the ideas of key theorists of cognitive development, with explanations of how developmental theories relate to early childhood education. An important cognitive skill during this stage is the ability to use language, so the chapter includes a section on how adults can teach language to children. Finally, we explore the social world of the young child, with an emphasis on the importance of peers and friends.

Between age two and age five, children change dramatically. *(Shutterstock)*

BODY GROWTH AND DEVELOPMENT

Between two and five years of age, the child's growth is fairly steady. Each year the child grows about 2 to 3 inches, and gains about 4 to 6 pounds. The body's proportions also change. During the first few years of life the child's head is huge compared to the rest of the body, and arms and legs are short and stubby. In fact, a common way toddlers drown is by falling into a tub, bucket, or toilet filled with water. Because their heads are large and heavy, toddlers often tumble head-first into things, and with short arms that do not reach above the head, it is impossible to for them to push themselves out of the water as an older child would do. As they grow, their torso, arms, and legs grow longer, and their tummies gets flatter; as compared to earlier years, the heads begin to look smaller

Beatrice, Melvin, Maja, and Lucas

Thirty-five-year-old Beatrice Magnusson and 34-year-old Melvin Malmer live together in Umeå, Sweden, with their children, 4-year-old Maja and 2-year-old Lucas. Umeå is a small city, situated about 250 miles south of the Arctic Circle. Winters are dark and cold; in summer, there is almost constant sunlight. Beatrice jokes, "There is no bad weather, just bad clothing."

Like many Swedish couples, Beatrice and Melvin are not married. Melvin explains, "After 7 years of living together we knew we wanted to have children, but we don't have strong religious beliefs so there was no need to marry."

A midwife assisted Beatrice during her pregnancies, and Beatrice says, "Everything was perfect." In Sweden birth is considered a natural process, and medical interventions are uncommon. Although medical care is free, doctors are seen only rarely during pregnancy or delivery, and for most women, a highly trained midwife assists with pregnancy and birth. Sweden consistently ranks first or second as one of the safest places in the world to give birth.

Beatrice is a university researcher, and Melvin is a high school teacher. When a child arrives Swedes get 390 days of parental leave at 80 percent of their usual salary. Because of this policy, most infants are with a parent rather than another caregiver. After Maja's birth both parents stayed home for 3 months and then returned to part-time work, an arrangement that allowed them to share childcare. Part-time counts half toward the 390 days of leave, and another 390 days were gained when Lucas was born. Beatrice and Melvin intend to continue part-time work for another six months.

While Lucas spends his days with a parent, Maja goes to a förskolan (preschool). Every neighborhood has a preschool center, regulated by national standards. Fees are based on family income, so it is affordable for all Swedish families. Beatrice says, "Of course the government should help families grow and do well. Good childcare is necessary for the survival of the country." Parents are entitled to paid vacation, plus 60 days a year at 80 percent salary if a child gets sick, but neither Maja nor Lucas has ever been sick.

Förskolan is for children between the ages of 1 and 5. At age 6 most children attend a transitional year that prepares them for formal schooling, which begins at 7 years of age. The emphasis in preschool is social, not academic. Melvin says, "It's important children play and learn from each other. They don't need

(continues)

(continued)
to learn letters and numbers at a specific time—some will be interested earlier than others." Beatrice adds, "The children learn about being honest and kind to each other. They participate in decisions, like, they vote on which snack to prepare."

An emphasis on justice, kindness, and fair play is not surprising—Sweden was the first country to ban spanking. Neither Beatrice nor Melvin see a need for spanking, "Sometimes the kids know they are misbehaving, and do it anyway. I am firm," Melvin says, "but, not physical. I use time-out or take away their toys." He adds, "Bea is not as firm. She says she has fewer rules, so the kids get away with more with her." Beatrice nods in agreement.

in proportion to the body. By the age of five, children can reach their arms over their head, with each arm able to touch the opposite ear.

Normative Growth

Arnold Gesell, first mentioned in Chapter 1, was influenced by psychologist G. Stanley Hall who believed in **maturation**—the idea that development occurs according to a naturally unfolding sequence. Gesell began his career working with developmentally disabled children; to better understand atypical development, he felt it was important to learn about normal development. Later, as a researcher he conducted cross-sectional studies comparing infants, preschoolers, and school-aged children. He looked at the mental, motor, language, and social abilities of children at different ages. Examining many children at each age revealed a picture of what was typical.

Based on Gesell's work, **norms** were created for many aspects of development, so children could be compared to these "norms" to see how they were growing. By today's standard's Gesell's studies were flawed because he did not study enough children, and the children he did study were from the same cultural and economic groups; nonetheless, he was the first scientist to make detailed observations of growth patterns, and his work was the foundation for measurement standards doctors use today.

Today, when children receive medical attention their growth is measured and compared with a **growth curve table,** a graph that shows averages of growth at different ages. Growth curves can be computed for physical attributes such as average height, weight, or head circumference, or for attributes such as language or intelligence. Sometimes there are different growth curves for boys and girls, or for children from different countries. Growth curve tables show that growth slows down during early childhood (compared to earlier years) but remains relatively steady.

Using a cross-sectional method to obtain averages of different children at different ages makes growth appear steady and constant. However, longitudinal studies that follow the same children over time show that children have **growth spurts**, periods of rapid growth in a short period of time (probably less than 24 hours) followed by a period of no growth (often weeks). So a child's growth follows a stop-and-start pattern. This explains why a child will fit into clothes or shoes one day, and might then grow out of them overnight.

DEVELOPMENT OF GROSS AND FINE MOTOR SKILLS

During early childhood gross motor skills make tremendous gains. At 2 years of age, children walk rhythmically, run, jump, and hop, but they are still a little unsteady. By 3 to 4 years of age, they will begin to gallop and pedal a tricycle, and by 5 to 6 years of age, they can skip, throw, and catch smoothly.

As the body becomes less top-heavy, the **center of gravity** shifts down toward the belly. The center of gravity is the place on the body where weight is equally divided above and below that point. If the head is very heavy compared to the rest of the body, the center of gravity will be high on the body. So the center of gravity for toddlers is very high on the chest. If hips, belly, and bottom are heavy compared to the rest of the body, the center of gravity will be low. During early childhood, the center of gravity is about the same as the center of the body, which makes it easy to balance the body. Walking, tumbling, and climbing become nimble.

Fine motor skills also show gains. Around 2 to 3 years of age, children can hold a crayon and a large button; they can also use a fork, and create drawings (usually scribbles). Around 3 years of age, a child will be able to draw a "tadpole person," a circle with two dots representing eyes and two long lines emanating from the circle representing legs and a body. By 4 children will begin using scissors, and at 5 most children can copy numbers and letters, tie a bow, and make more realistic "person" drawings, which will now include eyes, nose, mouth, belly-button, and five fingers on each hand.

Many of the advances in gross and fine motor skills are enabled by changes in the nervous system. For example, there are steady gains in coordination of the two sides of the body, so skipping, pedaling, and steering get easier; catching, lacing, and handing objects from one hand to the other also become steadier.

THE NERVOUS SYSTEM AND BRAIN DEVELOPMENT

The brain development that begins in earlier years continues throughout early childhood. At birth, the lower regions of the brain are largely developed. The **cortex**, the gray matter on the outside part of the brain, is where most of the changes occur after birth. The cortex is responsible for perception, body movement, thinking, language, and memory.

Fig. 4.1 Birth to 36 Months: Boys Length-for-age and Weight-for-age percentiles

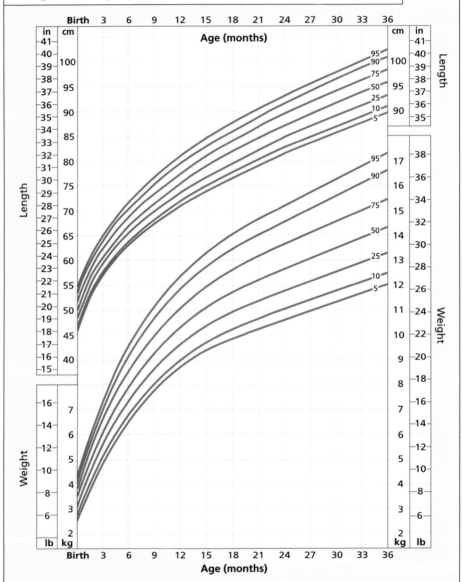

Source: Developed by the National Center for Health Statistics in collaboration with the National Center for Chronic Disease Prevention and Health Promotion, 2000. Available online. URL: http://www.cdc.gov/growthcharts.

© Infobase Learning

Fig. 4.2 Birth to 36 Months: Girls Length-for-age and Weight-for-age percentiles

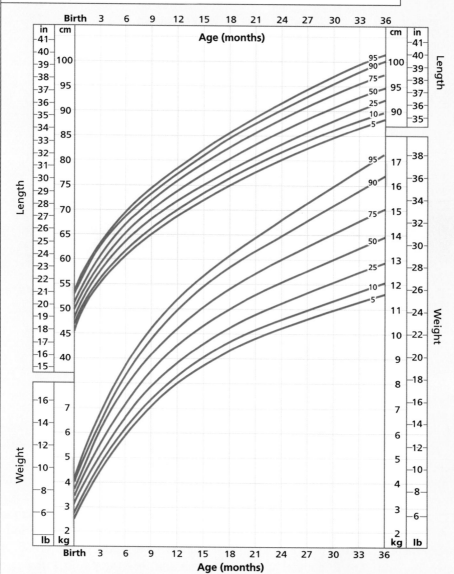

Source: Developed by the National Center for Health Statistics in collaboration with the National Center for Chronic Disease Prevention and Health Promotion, 2000. Available online. URL: http://www.cdc.gov/growthcharts.

Fig. 4.3 Basic Structure of the Brain

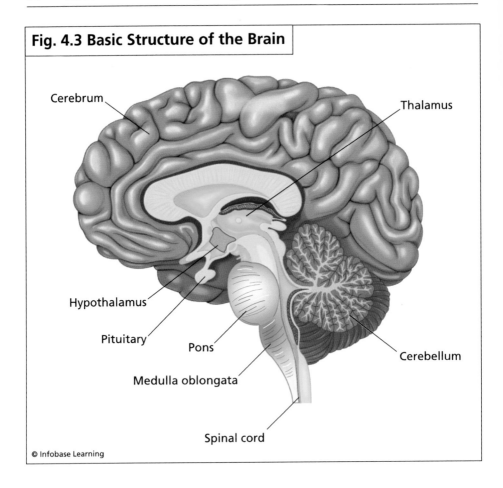

Cerebrum

Thalamus

Hypothalamus

Pituitary

Pons

Cerebellum

Medulla oblongata

Spinal cord

© Infobase Learning

Recall that between the ages 2 and 6 the brain goes from 20 percent of its adult weight to 90 percent, with the greatest change occurring in the cortex. Myelination accounts for some of the weight gain. In fact, an increase in myelin is especially noticeable in regions of the brain responsible for motor skills.

As growth spurts in the brain continue, there are periods of time when axons and dendrites rapidly grow to form synaptic connections, followed by periods when there is selective pruning of unused synapses. Overproduction of synapses gives the brain great potential and extra connections in case of future damage. However, pruning is also important because when there are too many neural pathways, the brain works more slowly, is inefficient, and uses more energy.

Brain Lateralization

One brain structure that experiences tremendous growth during early childhood is the **corpus callosum**, a bundle of nerve fibers that connect the left and right sides, or hemispheres, of the cortex. Communication between the hemispheres makes movement more coordinated and allows thinking on both sides of the brain to be more integrated.

The adult brain is **lateralized**, meaning each hemisphere has its own functions. In most people, for example, the left hemisphere is responsible for controlling the right side of the body, language, logic, and math, whereas the right hemisphere is responsible for the left side of the body, creativity, emotions, special perception, arts, and music. Lateralization appears to be largely determined by genetics, but experience also plays a role.

The young child's corpus callosum is not fully developed, therefore the hemispheres are not yet completely specialized. This is why a toddler might hold a spoon in one hand and a fork in the other and eat with both equally well. As the corpus callosum develops the brain becomes more lateralized, and one consequence is that by around the age of 5, children show a clear hand preference (about 85 percent are right handed).

COGNITIVE DEVELOPMENT

Two major theories of cognitive development are Swiss psychologist Jean Piaget's stage theory and Russian psychologist Lev Vygotsky's sociocultural theory. Both theorists were born in 1896 and developed their theories at about the same time. The theories differ primarily in their descriptions of how children learn; Piaget proposed children learn by seeking out information and experiences in the environment, whereas Vygotsky believed children learn through social interactions. Both theories have had a tremendous influence on the way contemporary psychologists understand cognitive development and on the field of education.

Piaget's Preoperational Thought

According to Piaget, the sensorimotor stage of cognitive development begins at birth and ends at 2 years of age. Children between the ages of 2 and 7 are in the **preoperational stage**. The stage after preoperational is concrete operations, which lasts from 7 to 11 years of age. The final stage, formal operations, begins around age 12. Understanding what *operation* means is helpful when trying to remember the correct order of Piaget's stages. An **operation** involves moving things around; it is a process or a series of steps. (Think about what it means when a car operates or when a doctor performs an operation—in both instances, parts are being moved around). When Piaget used the term operation, he referred to the ability to mentally move information around. So a 3-year-old is *pre*operational—not quite able to move information around in her or his head. The *concrete* operational 9-year-old can move concrete information around, and the *formal* operational 14-year-old can think about abstract things.

Accidents or Preventable Injuries

Early childhood is one of the most challenging times to keep children out of harm's way. They lack the experience to know what is safe and unsafe, they have the physical abilities to quickly get into all sorts of trouble, and they are curious about everything. This is particularly dangerous in children who also have an overactive and impulsive temperament (see Chapter 1).

Around the world, injuries cause millions of deaths among young children. In the United States about one-fourth of children under the age of 5 will have an accident that requires medical attention, and most injuries occur at home. Falls, poison, burns, choking, drowning, car accidents, and murder resulting from child abuse are some of the leading causes of death. But life-ending injuries are only a small part of the problem—many more injuries result in disability and hospitalization.

Public health experts dislike the word "accident" because calling injuries *accidental* implies the injury was unexpected and impossible to avoid. Most injuries in fact are not inevitable, and even in cases that are deemed "unavoidable," damage can be minimized if protective steps are taken. "Accidents" generally happen due to carelessness, a lack of knowledge, a lack of training, or a lack of understanding that something is risky.

Preventing injuries or minimizing the damage from them can be accomplished with "The 4 Es": Education, Enactment/Enforcement, Engineering, and Economic Incentives. Education raises awareness that something is a risk and also teaches how to minimize the risk. Usually such campaigns target an at-risk group of people. For example, the "Back to Sleep" campaign described in

Piaget said preoperational children do not simply know "more" than they knew when they were in the sensorimotor stage—they think differently. No longer do they use their senses and motor skills to understand the world, they now think about objects not currently present and use symbols, such as language. Another example of symbolic thought is the emergence of **make-believe play**—using one object to stand for another, such as holding a shoe to the ear to symbolize a phone or wearing a pot for a helmet.

The preoperational stage is often characterized by what children cannot do. For example, they lack **conservation**, the idea that the properties of an object stay the same, even if its appearance changes. If a researcher shows a 4-year-old child two tall, thin cups with the same amount of juice in each and points to each asking, "Does this cup have more, does that cup have more, or are they the same?" The child will correctly answer, "They are the same." But if the researcher takes one of the cups and pours the juice into a shorter, wider cup and asks the same question,

Chapter 3 was an effective educational campaign that targeted new parents and ultimately reduced deaths from SIDS. There have been many other successful educational campaigns, such as fire safety programs teaching preschoolers to "Stop-Drop-And-Roll."

Enactment involves passing (enacting) laws that promote safety, and enforcing the laws that already exist. Requiring children to ride in car seats, requiring pools to have fences around them, requiring pajama makers to make their products flame resistant, and requiring drug companies to sell medicine with safety caps are all examples of this strategy. Many laws are enacted and enforced locally, so the strength of the law and degree of enforcement vary tremendously from community to community and from state to state. However, health experts recognize that legislation has been the best way to reduce large numbers of injuries. In 1975 a number of children fell out of windows from public housing apartments; in 1976 New York City enacted a law requiring window guards. In 1977 the number of children falling from windows fell by half and continued to decline in subsequent years as adherence to the law increased. Similarly, when communities pass a law requiring fencing around swimming pools, rates of childhood drowning typically drop about 90 percent.

Engineering involves making the environment safer. Building cars with anti-lock breaks, painting lines on roads, designing stronger bike helmets, and using mulch or shredded rubber on playgrounds are all ways to engineer a safer environment. Finally, when there are economic incentives to obey laws, adherence increases. For example, when businesses get fined for selling alcohol to underage drinkers, underage drinking declines.

the child will point to the short wide cup and answer, "This one has more." The researcher can then ask, "But did I add any, did I take any away?" and the child will respond "No, but it still has more." The child does not understand that the amount of liquid is *conserved*, and it did not change despite a change in appearance. Pour the juice back into the original cup and the child will say, "Now it's the same again."

But this does not only happen with liquids. Showing a child two balls of clay and then smooshing one down into a pancake, or showing a child two lines of 5 candies and then spreading the candies in one of the lines far apart, reveals that preoperational children use **centration**, meaning that they focus on the most salient aspect of the problem (e.g., only focus on height, or only focus on width). They do not **decenter** and focus on two or more dimensions of the problem—they do not consider height and width.

Also contributing to their answers is that they do not use **reversibility**—mentally undoing steps. Older children on the cusp of acquiring conservation, such as a 5-year-old, might suggest you pour the juice back to get the same again. But younger children cannot mentally reverse steps.

Classification of objects can also be difficult. Not until about the age of 4 can children sort a pile of objects by color, size, or shape, and even older preoperational children struggle with classes and subclasses of objects. For example, preoperational children are unable to correctly answer the question, "If I have 6 oranges and 3 apples, which do I have more of, apples or fruit?"

Piaget believed young children to be **egocentric**—they view the world from their own perspective and cannot adopt another point of view. He illustrated egocentrism with the three-mountain task. He allowed children to look at a table with three plaster mountains of different sizes: one with a snow-capped peak, one with a cross on top, and one with a house on it. He then placed a doll directly opposite of where a child stood and asked the child to select from a set of pictures what the doll saw. Younger children picked the picture of the view they themselves saw; older children picked what the doll would see. Piaget concluded that when children first acquire the ability to mentally represent things, they assume others have the same perceptions, thoughts, and feelings. So 4-year-olds will hold up a picture and say, "Look at my picture," not understanding that the viewer sees the back of the picture. The child will also assume if he likes the picture, others will too.

Contemporary Views of Preoperational Thought

For decades researchers have studied Piaget's ideas about young children. Most research supports Piaget's belief that the thoughts of young children are often tied to what they can perceive, and they do not always understand the logic behind things such as conservation. However, many researchers have argued that Piaget's original tests for children were too complicated, and children do not fall neatly into individual stages.

Contemporary research indicates young children can do better on Piaget's tests when those tests are simplified, and children understand more than Piaget thought. For example, rather than using the three-mountain task to demonstrate egocentrism, researcher John Flavell showed preschoolers a card with a dog on one side and a cat on the other. The card was then held up between the child and researcher. When children were asked what the researcher could see, they performed perfectly (Flavell, Everett, Croft, & Flavell, 1981). Additionally, there has been evidence that children acquire skills earlier than Piaget thought. In another study Flavell showed children a sponge painted to look like a rock. When asked what it was, some 3-year-olds said it was a sponge, others said it was a rock; 4- and 5-year-olds said it was a sponge that looked like a rock. Older children considered several pieces of information about the object—an ability Piaget did not believe preoperational children had.

Vygotsky's Sociocultural Theory

According to Vygotsky, humans are social creatures; therefore, human learning takes place in the context of social interactions. To understand human learning, scientists must look at children in their natural environment—removing them and studying them in an artificial laboratory gives an artificial picture of what they know. So, he studied children in their own natural worlds, surrounded by adults and peers, and when he considered cognitive development he looked at what children could do with the assistance of others in their environment. This approach views cognitive development as a result of give-and-take process between a child and others.

In Vygotsky's model, the child is an apprentice, and the adult or more mature peer is the mentor. Children learn through **guided participation.** Mentors present learners with work that is challenging yet attainable, help and provide instruction if needed, and encourage and motivate the learners. Parents, teachers, and children who have already mastered a skill can all serve as mentors. So learning begins in a social situation, and as a skill is acquired, it becomes increasingly internalized.

But the potential for learning depends on the **zone of proximal development**—the range of skills that can be learned with the assistance of a mentor. This range is greater than what can be learned alone. Students do not learn when given easy problems that require no effort, nor do they learn if given a task too far beyond what they are capable. But when mentors present realistic challenges and then provide a supportive environment, children learn earlier and will move to a higher level of mental functioning.

To support learning, mentors use **scaffolding**. They break tasks down into manageable pieces, provide material or hints if needed, offer encouragement, and then gradually remove these supports as a task is mastered (just like painters need physical scaffolding to reach the top of a building and then need less and less as they complete the job). Done correctly, the child is constantly challenged, supported when necessary, and acquires confidence from repeated successes.

For example, imagine 4-year-old Maja picks up a 24-piece puzzle and asks her father Melvin for help putting it together. Melvin looks at the pieces and says, "Where should we start?" Maja picks up random pairs to see if they match and answers, "Put together pieces that match." Melvin suggests, "How about we turn the pieces face-up to start." As they turn the pieces over Melvin points out various colors on the pieces. Maja suggests, "Let's make piles of colors." Melvin agrees, and then connects a few of the pieces with straight edges. As Melvin observes, Maja connects straight-edged pieces of similar colors until the entire outer rim is complete. She then works on the inner pieces. Occasionally Melvin asks, "Are you sure those colors go together?" After a few minutes the puzzle is done, and Melvin asks if Maja wants to try an even larger puzzle. She enthusiastically agrees.

Putting together an entire puzzle can be overwhelming. To make it less overwhelming, Melvin broke the task into small steps, such as making piles and working on the edge. He provided assistance when needed, but also simply observed when things were going well. Finally, to prevent too much frustration, he intervened when his daughter made errors. He then suggested a more challenging task when appropriate. There was constant give and take between the two.

For Vygotsky, language was a tool necessary for thought. Thought and language develop together, and children think differently once they begin thinking with words. Vygotsky identified three stages of children's language use. At first language is social and used to communicate. Next, children use **private speech** to manage their own thinking. Children talk out loud or whisper to themselves as an aid to solve problems or direct behavior. Adults occasionally use private speech, but it is most common during early childhood. Eventually private speech stays internal, and out loud private speech diminishes as children become more cognitively mature. The final stage is when children use inner speech to form verbal thoughts that guide thinking and actions. At every point, language drives cognitive development.

Contemporary Views of Vygotsky's Theory
Until about 30 years ago, Vygotsky's work was known only in Russia, so much of the research on the theory remained unknown to Western psychologists. In the United States, there are several topics, such as private speech, that have more research support than others. The major criticism of Vygotsky's theory is the direct opposite of the major criticism of Piaget's theory. Piaget is criticized for focusing too much on the individual's maturation and not attending to the influence of environment. Vygotsky's theory has been criticized for focusing too much on the social world and not enough on what individuals construct on their own.

Piaget's and Vygotsky's Contributions to Education
Piaget and Vygotsky both made many contributions to the field of education. Piaget's stage theory clearly illustrated how materials and learning strategies should match a child's stage or ability level. Because children actively construct their own knowledge, the teacher's role is to provide learning opportunities and direct the child toward those opportunities. Preoperational children who lack mental operations need teachers to give hands-on learning activities, break instructions into small steps, provide demonstrations, use repetition, and then step back and allow children to explore on their own.

In contrast, according to Vygotsky's theory, the teacher should be an active part of a student's education, scaffolding learning situations, and making sure students have the tools needed for learning. Most importantly, the teacher structures learning situations so students teach each other, having the opportunity to be both mentors and apprentices.

LANGUAGE DEVELOPMENT

Both Vygotsky and Piaget recognized the importance of language development, particularly during early childhood, and increasing evidence from brain researchers indicates that early childhood is a *sensitive period* for learning a first language (see Chapter 3).

The **naming explosion** that began during the toddler years, continues during early childhood and expands to include verbs, adverbs, and adjectives. Parents often wonder how children learn so many words in such a short time. The explanation is **fast-mapping**, a quick way to link words together in mental categories based on a given situation. Using this, children learn words that they have only heard a few times—they guess the meaning of a word based on the context. For example, a mother says, "Would you like a magic bar? Look, it's a cookie shaped like a bar." She hands the treat to the child and says, "Yummy, I love magic bars." In this example several words are linked together; "magic bar" is now placed into the "cookie" category, along with "yummy" and "love." So the next time grandpa says "I love you," the child might ask, "Like a magic bar?"

Not surprisingly, the more children are spoken to, the more words they know. Similarly, when caregivers use **child-directed speech** and adjust their language to the child's ability, children learn more quickly. In the magic-bar example, the mother used short sentences, lots of repetition, and mostly words the child was familiar with. These strategies assist in learning a language.

As 2- and 3-year-olds begin combining words into simple sentences, it is interesting to note that they do not merely repeat sentences heard before. They create new sentences and apply the basic rules of their language. One way researchers know children are not repeating what they heard before is that they make mistakes an adult would not make, and their mistakes follow the rules of their language. For example, one rule in English is to add an *s* to make the word plural; another rule is to add *ed* to change a word to the past tense. But there are exceptions to these rules, and when children apply rules to the exceptions, it is evidence that they know the rules. The child might say, "I saw lots of mouses" (instead of *mice*), or "I runned fast." (instead of *ran*). Parents worry their child is speaking incorrectly, when they should actually be pleased the child knows the rule. Applying grammatical rules to the exceptions is called **overregulation**—overusing the rules of regular words.

INFANT, TODDLER, AND EARLY CHILDHOOD CARE AND EDUCATION

As children get older, they tend to spend more time away from parents and more time in formal care and educational settings. In the United States, most children between the ages of 2 and 5 spend at least some time with caregivers other than parents. The rates of non-parental care for children under the age of 2 are lower,

Pervasive Developmental Disorders

A Pervasive Developmental Disorder (PDD) is a group of disorders that involve delayed development of social and communication skills. Usually a PDD is identified in children around the age of 3, but symptoms may begin earlier. There are many types of PDDs, such as **Autism, Rett's Syndrome**, and **Asperger's Syndrome**. Symptoms vary, but might include problems speaking or understanding language, relating to people or objects in unusual ways, obsession with routine, or repeating movements. In some children symptoms are severe; in others they are mild. Similarly, intelligence and degree of impairment can vary.

In the 1950s and 1960s doctors thought cold or distant parents caused PDDs and called mothers of autistic children **refrigerator mothers**. The treatment was to remove children from their parents. But the doctors were horribly wrong. The treatment did not work, and a generation of parents and children were mistreated as a result of this ignorance. Today, there is an abundance of evidence that poor parenting does not cause PDDs.

Although the cause of PDDs remains unknown, there is a clear connection to the brain. But exactly what is happening in the brain is unknown. Additionally, because PDDs can run in families, there is some evidence of a genetic predisposition. As of now, however, there is no cure and no known method of prevention.

and vary tremendously from country to country. In countries where the cost of care is subsidized by the government (e.g., Sweden, Netherlands and France), rates of enrollment are high, and the quality of childcare also is high. However, in many parts of the world (e.g., Malawi and India), there are few options for formal daycare, so rates are very low. In the United States most families are responsible for the entire cost of childcare. Nonetheless, rates of non-parental care for infants and toddlers are high, with approximately 50 percent of children under 9 months of age, 65 percent of children under 3 years of age, and 85 percent of children between 3 and 5 years of age in at least some non-parental care situation.

Non-parental care of young children has many names. For example, care for infants and toddlers is called daycare, babysitting, family care; education during early childhood is called preschool, nursery school, daycare. These names usually convey little about the programs themselves and can be misleading. The following section will emphasize what is important about early care.

Infant and Toddler Care in the United States

During the last few decades there has been a great deal of research on the effects of non-parental care for infants and toddlers, but general conclusions have been difficult to draw. The biggest problem is that most studies use convenience samples, such as children of professors who attend a high-quality daycare center

Because the symptoms of PDDs vary tremendously, treatment approaches also vary. Children with PDDs usually require a **program of intervention**, not just one treatment. So parents, teachers, health care providers, speech therapists, occupational therapists, physical therapists, and counselors might all work together with the family to address different issues. On the whole, the most successful treatment approach is one-on-one behavioral therapy offering rewards and punishments to change social and communication behaviors. Some children with PDDs can attend school in a regular classroom with minimal supports, whereas others need a special classroom. Some children with PDDs exhibit severe behavior problems and can benefit from medication to treat these behavior problems.

The long-term prognosis of children with PDDs is difficult to predict. Generally, children who begin with fewer symptoms have a better long-term prognosis. But, despite treatment, some children will get worse as they age while others will improve. Some will live independently as adults; others will require tremendous support. Earlier and more intensive behavioral interventions tend to be more successful. Brain researchers, in an effort to better treat, prevent, and cure PDD, are working to identify what is happening inside the brains of individuals with a PDD.

associated with a university. It is difficult to know what would happen if those same children were placed in a poor-quality care situation. But no parents would volunteer to have their children randomly assigned into poor-quality care or, for that matter, even into high-quality care. So for most research, family characteristics, such as parents' education, family income, and parent age, are often linked to characteristics of the daycare situation, including factors such as quality of care and number of hours in care.

In an effort to address the weaknesses of previous research and conduct a single comprehensive study, the National Institute of Child Health and Human Development (NICHD)[1] gathered a group of researchers to design and conduct the NICHD Study of Early Child Care (SECC). Beginning in 1991 a diverse sample of 1,364 newborns and their families were recruited at 10 locations across the country. Researchers studied the children and their families mostly in their natural environments at regular intervals, beginning at birth. The researchers conducted observations and testing; and family members, caregivers, and teachers participated in interviews and responded to questionnaires. Many aspects of child and family development were mea-

---

[1] The NICHD is part of the U.S. Department of Health and Human Services and conducts and supports research in the developmental sciences.

sured. The research was intended to be long range and has continued to this day. Because the same children have been studied over and over, this is a longitudinal study.

Having such a large number of diverse children makes it possible to look at various types of situations. But with so many children and so many variables all in one study, the results are complicated. In general, in the first two years of life, the quality and quantity of childcare was important. Regardless of type of care, whether with mother, a grandmother, daycare center, babysitter, etc., children in high-quality care performed better on cognitive, language, and reading tests when they began kindergarten. The NICHD research also found that children in more than 30 hours of non-maternal childcare a week had poorer social development than children in less non-maternal care. But, parents played an important role. For example, mothers with more education and mothers who were more responsive to their children were more likely to place those children in high-quality care situations. Overall, the quality of parenting had a much greater long-term impact on children than the quality of childcare.

Early Childhood Care and Education
During the past few decades, extensive research has examined the effects of education during early childhood. Consistently, high-quality care has been linked to school readiness and positive social skills. In contrast, low-quality education does not have the same lasting benefits. Surveys of kindergarten teachers show that children who do not attend quality preschool, regardless of economic background, have a significant disadvantage in kindergarten.

High-quality care includes highly trained teachers, a low child-teacher ratio, regular one-on-one child-teacher interactions, responsive teachers, opportunities for gross and fine motor exploration, and all of this occurring in a safe and welcoming environment. Good teachers use play and everyday experiences as opportunities for instruction, and allow for both child- and teacher-initiated activities.

Consistently, state licensed daycare or preschool proves to be better than unregulated care; however, simply meeting state regulations does not ensure high quality. Schools accredited by the *National Association for the Education of Young Children* have met higher standards and tend to be high in quality. Some warning signs of poor quality care are a high teacher turnover, rigid rules about when parents can visit, children who appear bored, and no educational philosophy.

When parents select a child care environment, they consider many things, including convenience of location and hours, cost, and educational philosophy. Some communities have more options available than others. Usually an early childhood educational philosophy falls into one of three categories: academic, developmental, and intervention.

Academic programs stress a traditional teacher-led ready-to-learn curriculum. Teachers structure the children's learning of letters, numbers, colors, and shapes through formal lessons and repetition. The day is divided into time periods for academics, center-based play, creative arts, gross-motor play, and quiet time. This highly structured learning environment is successful at preparing many children for school; however, there are concerns that this style undermines motivation, particularly in very active or imaginative children.

In **developmental programs** most learning is individually directed and takes place during play. Piaget's influence is evident in that developmentally appropriate materials are provided and children are encouraged to explore and discover at their own pace. Vygotsky's influence is also evidence because developmental classrooms often have children of various abilities or ages working together, thereby reflecting the mentor-apprentice relationship. For example, **Montessori Schools** promote Piaget's idea of the child as a little scientist. Children choose their own activities, and their activities are viewed as "work" rather than play. But materials are designed to promote exploration; for example, children "work" with sandpaper letters, so "work" for the child feels like play. In addition, Montessori Schools emphasize social justice, and children are taught to cooperate and take responsibility for their actions.

Intervention programs are designed to help children who are at risk of being delayed to catch up to their peers. The most well-known intervention program, **Head Start**, began in 1965 and is a federally funded program that provides poor children with preschool, adequate nutrition, dental, and health services; it requires that parents participate by contributing to program planning, working in the classroom, or attending adult programs. Although federally funded, Head Start schools are locally controlled, so some Head Start classrooms adopt an academic philosophy and others adopt a developmental philosophy. What is unique about intervention programs like Head Start is that they are concerned with every aspect of child development: physical, cognitive, and social.

Unfortunately, there are not enough Head Start classrooms to serve all children who qualify, so there are long waiting lists. Selection is random. Research comparing children who got into Head Start and children who were not selected showed Head Start graduates had better prereading skills, such as knowledge about letters and colors, and had fewer behavior problems. In other long-term studies of intervention programs, long-term benefits were astounding. Compared to peers who were not involved in such programs, intervention children were less likely to be placed in special education, less likely to be held back in school, less likely to have an early pregnancy, less likely to be delinquent, more likely to graduate high school, and more likely to find and keep employment. Of course, intervention programs are very costly, but

A child learns phonograms in a Montessori school. *(Wikipedia)*

social scientists believe the long-term financial benefits to society far outweigh the significant short-term cost.

SOCIAL AND EMOTIONAL DEVELOPMENT

As mentioned at the start of this chapter, many refer to the 2 to 5 year age period as the play years. As physical skills and cognitive skills change, children's play takes on a whole new dynamic, and many developmentalists argue that play is the most important job of children during early childhood.

At the same time that children become more aware of their own wants and abilities, they also begin to better understand the thoughts and feelings of others. This is the foundation of **friendships**, which most children form during early childhood. First friends tend to be same-age and same-sex peers. Compared to interaction with other classmates, interactions between friends tend to be more complex; they fight more, but are also better at compromising.

Play

While playing, children use fine and gross motor skills. They interact socially, they make and execute plans, they use language, and they learn to regulate their emotions. Play is important because it enhances just about every aspect of development: cognitive, language, creativity, fine and gross-motor, and social and emotional.

In the early 1930s, sociologist Mildred Parten observed 42 children aged 2 to 5. Based on her observations, she classified play into 6 categories. **Unoccupied play** occurs when the child is not playing, but may occasionally glance at others playing. **Onlooker** behavior occurs when the child watches and interacts, but is not an active part of the play. In **solitary play** the child plays alone and makes no effort to engage others. **Parallel play** is when children are engaged in similar activities, but play independently. They are near each other and pay attention to each other, but do not try to influence each other. **Associative play** occurs when children play similarly, share materials, and talk to each other about their play but do not coordinate games or activities. They are clearly interested in each other but not in the other's activities. **Cooperative play** occurs among a group of children who have a common goal with a clear division of roles among group members, such as role-playing, teacher and student, or a more formal game of tag.

According to Parten (1932), younger children are more likely to engage in non-social play, such as solitary or parallel play; as language and social skills mature, play is more likely to be more social, such as associative and cooperative

Revisiting Beatrice, Melvin, Maja, and Lucas

Swedes like Beatrice and Melvin pay high taxes to fund their social services, such as free medical care, generous parental leave, and subsidized childcare, but the taxes in Sweden are not much higher than those paid by people living in the United States. Swedes pay a maximum tax of 50 percent; in the United States, the maximum tax is 42 percent. Both Melvin and Beatrice think it is worth it. "I wouldn't want it any other way," Beatrice says. "We pay high taxes, but we get everything we need. And it is fair. A person with a low-paying job gets the same benefits as a person with a high-paying job."

There is evidence that Beatrice and Melvin's life-satisfaction level is typical of other Swedes. Research shows that life in Sweden offers a greater degree of work-life balance and a greater degree of happiness. In 2006, British researcher Adrian White analyzed data from more than 100 studies about happiness. He ranked life satisfaction of about 80,000 adults worldwide and found Denmark ranked number 1, Sweden number 7, the United States number 24, the United Kingdom 41, Cuba 83, and Russia number 167. Melvin and Beatrice both say, "This is the best place in the world to live," but Beatrice adds, "except for the long nights of February."

play. Although there have been a number of efforts to redefine play, contemporary researchers continue to support Parten's classifications. However, there has been some debate as to whether or not there is a developmental sequence of play, as she suggested. Researchers agree that children need play, and lots of it. It is what they prefer most, and what they do best.

CONCLUSION

After the first two years, physical growth slows down in early childhood, but remarkable motor and cognitive gains continue, largely due to maturation in the brain. Experience is still important for good brain development—one of the most impressive accomplishments during early childhood, for example, is the rapid acquisition of language, which is largely determined by how much language children are exposed to. Although formal instruction is not required, human interactions are. Increasingly children are exposed to caregivers other than their parents, and the quality of this care is linked to later cognitive development. Children also spend more time with peers. As the next chapter will show, these playful interactions can shape the foundation for later social skills.

Further Reading

Centers for Disease Control and Prevention. Available at http://www.cdc.gov/
National Association for the Education of Young Children. Available at http://www.naeyc
    .org/
National Head Start Association. Available at http://www.nhsa.org/
NICHD Early Child Care Research Network. "Early Child Care and Children's Development Prior to School Entry: Results from the NICHD Study of Early Child Care. *American Educational Research Journal* 39 (2002): 133–164.
Schwartz, Casey. "Why It's Smart to Be Bilingual: The Brain's Real Super-food May Be Learning New Languages." *Newsweek* (August 7, 2011). Accessed August 1, 2011; available from http://www.thedailybeast.com/newsweek/2011/08/07/why-it-s-smart-to-be-bilingual.html

CHAPTER 5

DEVELOPMENT
DURING MIDDLE CHILDHOOD

AGE SIX TO AGE TWELVE

The earliest memories of most adults are about things that happened during middle childhood—playing with friends, incidents in elementary school, watching a favorite television show, or time with family. This chapter describes the physical, cognitive, social, and emotional development that occurs during middle childhood. It examines special issues, such as obesity, maltreatment, and losing the first tooth, as well as basic aspects of development, like brain and cognitive development. It will also cover psychometrics, standardized tests, and standards-based education. The chapter concludes with a discussion on the influence of parents and siblings during middle childhood, with descriptions of how family structure and family functioning impact development.

Middle childhood, also referred to as the school-years, occurs when children are 6 to 12 years old. Compared to younger children, school-age children are bigger, stronger, better coordinated, think in more complex ways, and are more socially mature. Comparing the experiences of Patrick, Gerard, and James highlights some of these differences. For 12-year-old Patrick, communication was of vital importance to getting along with peers. In contrast, it was less important for 8 year-old Gerard and five-year old James whose peers just wanted a playmate. There were also differences in the boys' understanding of life in Spain. James, just on the cusp between early childhood and middle childhood, created his own understanding of the written language in a very concrete

The DeStefanos in Spain

Marie and Steve and their sons, 12-year-old Patrick, 8-year-old Gerard, and 5-year-old James, moved to Spain for 6 months. They lived in Oviedo, the capital city of Asturias, a province in northern Spain. Once they had settled in, the boys were enrolled in a public school. In the United States, the boys' took a bus to school and were in school from 9:00 a.m. to 3:00 p.m. The school day included supervised lunch and recess. In Spain, they walked to school at 9:00 a.m. and walked home at 2:00 p.m. Throughout Spain, schools and businesses close between 2:00 and 5:00 so families can share their midday meal. At 5:00 p.m. the boys returned to school for sports activities. Recess was also different—in Oviedo the entire school population spilled onto the playground at the same time, and teachers let children settle their own disputes. Physical fights occurred daily, with no teacher intervention. This was particularly surprising to Patrick who noticed, "In Spain, where there is a king, kids get in trouble for calling someone a bastard, but don't get in trouble for punching. At home nobody cares what you say, but you get in trouble for fighting."

Patrick, an outgoing preteen, had a difficult time being accepted by his classmates who had been together since early childhood. At first, his only friends were other immigrants. He worked hard to learn Spanish, and as his language

way—if it was cursive it was Spanish. But Patrick struggled to make sense of the cultural differences he encountered, and he concluded that the different views of misbehavior could best be explained by considering the history of each country. Clearly, this understanding is more complex than James'.

BODY GROWTH AND DEVELOPMENT

Between 6 and 12 years of age growth is slow and steady. Until the age of 8, boys are slightly heavier and taller than girls, but around the age of 9, girls have a growth spurt and become heavier and taller. Differences in height and weight are also influenced by variations in nutrition, health care, and genetics.

Bones and Teeth

During middle childhood most of the bones in the body lengthen. Activity and good nutrition are both important to bone growth. Muscles grow to adapt to longer bones; ligaments take longer to firmly attach themselves to the longer bones. Consequently, children are more flexible than adults, and it is easier for them to do flips and backbends.

Growth of facial bones, such as jaw and chin bones, allow for the loss of "baby" (primary) teeth as "adult" (permanent) teeth push in. On average, children skills improved, his classmates began to accept him. He eventually made Spanish friends when he joined a team playing a sport he knew well, but the Spanish kids did not—basketball.

In contrast, 8 year-old Gerard had an easy time making friends. Using gestures and a smile he participated in discussions and games where he understood nothing, but his peers did not mind his silence. One day the school called Marie because Gerard was sick. When she arrived at the school, he was fine. He had simply fallen asleep. He was bored because he couldn't understand the language. When he awoke, his teacher noticed that his cheeks were flushed and asked, in Spanish, if he were ill. Like any good student who doesn't know what he is being asked, Gerard answered "Si."

The youngest brother, James, did well in kindergarten. He was naturally quiet, and he used gestures to be understood. After a few weeks in school he came home to tell Marie he knew how to write his name in English and Spanish. He showed her his name printed "in English" and in cursive "Spanish." Because children in Oviedo learn to write in cursive before they learn how to print, James concluded that cursive must be Spanish.

The family's months abroad changed them all. Later in this chapter, you'll read Gerard's perception of the move to Spain.

lose their first tooth at 5 or 6 years of age and lose their last primary tooth between age 11 and 12. The first tooth lost is an exciting milestone often marked with a ritual. In Korea, children throw the tooth on the roof for a bird to pick up; in South Africa, a mouse picks up the tooth; and in Mongolia, the tooth is fed to a dog. Only in Western cultures does a child put a lost tooth under the pillow so a tooth fairy can leave money in place of the tooth. In each case, however, the children receive the gift of a strong permanent tooth.

Oral health varies from nation to nation and is closely linked to economics. Many poor children, particularly those in developing nations, have inadequate dental care or get none at all. In developing nations 90 percent of cavities go untreated, often leading to more serious problems. In Western countries, diets high in sugar are the primary contributor to tooth decay. In the United States tooth decay is the leading chronic infectious disease.

Development of Gross and Fine Motor Skills

Improved eye-hand coordination, quicker reaction times, and an increased ability to smoothly use multiple body parts leads to dramatic improvements in gross motor skills. Combine those skills with improved flexibility, greater muscle strength, and better balance, it is no surprise children are so adapt at running, climbing, jumping, and riding a bike. Fine motor skills also mature. Tasks such as using a screwdriver and writing steadily improve. Recall 5 year-old James could write in both print and cursive.

The Nervous System and Brain Development

Brain development continues during middle childhood. A thicker corpus callosum and increased myelination mean the brain begins to work more quickly. **Reaction time** refers to how long it takes to respond to something, and demonstrates how quickly the brain works. How long, for example, does it take to move away from a ball flying at one's face? To jump out of the way of a speeding car? To answer a question? To see something on a screen and press a button?

One way psychologists test reaction time is by measuring fingertip reaction by dropping a ruler between open fingers without warning. The amount of time it takes to react to the drop is measured by how far the ruler falls and where the

The Dark Side of Growth and Development: Childhood Obesity

According to the Centers for Disease Control childhood obesity has more than tripled in the past 30 years. In 1980, 6.5 percent of U.S. children between the ages of 6 and 11 were obese; by 2008 that rate was 19.6 percent. For children in the 12 to 19 year range, obesity rates went from 5 percent to 18.1 percent.

Fewer than a quarter of U.S. children eat the recommended 5 servings of fruits and vegetables a day; most children in fact do not even eat 2 servings. According to a 2009 National Youth Risk Survey, one-third of American children watch more than 3 hours of television a day, and two-thirds do not attend daily physical education classes. Globally, rates of obesity are also rising. Childhood obesity is considered an epidemic because it has increased and spread so quickly.

The cause of obesity is simple—more calories are eaten than burned. How much work it takes to burn calories is related to one's metabolism. **Metabolism** refers to the chemical reactions that take place inside cells, converting calories into the energy a body needs to work. Many things influence metabolism, including age, amount of muscle, activity level, and genetics. Most overweight children became overweight by consuming too many calories and not engaging in enough activity. In a small fraction of children, obesity is caused or exacerbated by other health problems.

For children, the physical consequences related to obesity include sleep apnea, joint problems, and respiratory problems. Overweight kids are also more likely to be ostracized, teased and bullied, which can lead to psychological problems like poor self-esteem, depression, and anxiety. These issues can fingers catch it. Research shows reaction time gets quicker and quicker from infancy until the late 20s, but then gradually slows down until the mid-50s. Between 50 and 70 there is not much change, but then reaction time slows dramatically after the age of 70.

COGNITIVE DEVELOPMENT
Middle childhood is when children in all cultures are expected to learn the skills they will need as adults. Many theoretical approaches examine cognitive development during middle childhood; this chapter considers the Piagetian and psychometric approaches to cognitive development.

Piaget's Concrete Thought
According to Piaget, the stage of concrete operations lasts from about age 7 to age 11, when mental abilities become more logical with respect to concrete

encourage already existing patterns of inactivity and overeating, thereby creating a dangerous cycle.

It is important to note that children become overweight within the context of a family. Parents supply food and model how to eat. (Raw veggies or potato chips? Meals whenever or on a relatively stable schedule?) Moreover, families set up the environment and thus provide opportunities for activity or inactivity. Some parents encourage outdoor play and limit electronic time (television, computer, electronic games); others place electronics in a child's bedroom, encouraging inactivity. It is generally parents, not children, who decide whether to walk or drive, use steps or an elevator, go biking or to a movie. Preventing kids from becoming overweight requires that the whole family engage in physical activity and eat healthy foods.

Once gained, weight is not easy to lose. Many children and families turn to adult treatments, such as weight control drugs, diets that limit or eliminate one type of food, or surgery. These were neither designed for nor proven safe for children. Research shows successful long-term weight loss involves taking weight off slowly by changing eating and activity habits. Because children are still growing it is often recommended that rather than strive for weight loss, the goal should be to prevent additional weight gain, so with time the child gains height and eventually grows in to her or his weight.

Some families focus attention on their overweight children, admonishing them by saying, "You should not eat that" and "You should exercise more." This approach is ineffective, demoralizing, and unfair (in most cases, the child became obese because the family's habits and routine aided and abetted this condition). Children have more success losing weight when all family members, regardless of body size, make healthy lifestyle changes.

things—that is, things that are real, solid, and visible. The preoperational child sees the world from an egocentric perspective, but the concrete child exhibits more objective and scientific thinking, and solves problems logically. Many mental operations that were challenging for the preoperational child are now mastered. For example, concrete operational children have no problems with conservation and reversibility. They understand a change in appearance does not necessarily mean that underlying characteristics change. For example, they know when a boy puts on a Halloween costume and looks like an old witch, he is still a boy. The concrete child can mentally reverse the steps that caused the change and see the original state.

Another skill preoperational children lack, but that concrete children have, is classification. During middle childhood children can easily sort objects, such as sorting stuffed animals into piles of white, brown, and spotted. Concrete children also understand **class inclusion,** where one group is part of a larger group. They recognize that some white stuffed animals are bears and some are cats.

Piaget clearly demonstrated that children are able to mentally hold and process several pieces of information at the same time. He showed, in fact, that school-age children consistently use logic. On the other hand, their logic is limited because they apply it only to concrete things. For example, they understand that 3 x 4 = 12, because these numbers can translate into concrete objects, such as 3 piles with 4 apples in each pile. But the idea of solving for x when the equation is $x - 4 = 8$ is more challenging. This problem requires imagining something abstract. In this example x is not concrete. In the next and final stage, formal operations, abstract thinking becomes evident.

Contemporary views of concrete thought

Piaget's theory provides a general description of how children think at different developmental stages. Contemporary researchers have mostly found support for his descriptions of concrete operations; however, modified methods of assessment can lead to children exhibiting logic at a younger age than Piaget thought possible. Hence, the shift from preoperational to concrete operations appears to occur gradually, not as a distinct stage.

Piaget has also been criticized because of the link between formal education and concrete operations. Compared to children without formal schooling, children with formal schooling perform better on Piaget's traditional tests of logic; however, this problem is minimized when tests more closely resemble real life. For example, psychologist Geoffrey Saxe interviewed 23 boys with little formal education, all of whom were 10 to 12 years old and sold candy in Brazil. He compared these middle childhood vendors to similarly aged non-vendor boys with the same level of education. He found both groups had difficulty identifying written numbers and solving problems on paper; all the boys would have failed a traditional mathematics test. However, both groups developed their own non-traditional ways of representing large numbers. The candy sellers developed their own understanding of arithmetic and ratio; they could quickly compute sales and gave correct change without writing anything on paper. Thus, they possessed the logic necessary to complete math problems, but were unable to demonstrate it in a traditional manner.

Psychometric Approach

The goal of the **psychometric approach** is to measure (metric) individual differences on various psychological traits (psycho). The basic assumption is that individuals differ with respect to how much of some trait they possess. Intelligence is one cognitive trait measured using the psychometric approach. Intelligence tests are used to determine how much individuals differ on the hypothesized psychological trait called intelligence.

Intelligence and Intelligence Tests

There are many definitions of **intelligence,** and little agreement about what intelligence is. Most agree that intelligence enables people to think, plan, and solve problems. But beyond that, there is little agreement. Some posit that intelligence is one general thing or factor, arguing that individuals who score high on a mathematics test also tend to score high on a language test.

Others posit that more than one type of intelligence exists. According to this perspective, street intelligence and classroom intelligence are two distinct kinds of intelligence. Support for this perspective might be the Brazilian street children studied by Geoffrey Saxe—they exhibited high knowledge of street math but lower levels of school math. One advocate of the concept of **multiple intelligences** is Howard Gardner who posits that each type of intelligence represents a distinct ability. Gardner, in fact, identified linguistic, logical-mathematical, spatial, musical, bodily-kinesthetic, interpersonal, intrapersonal, and naturalistic intelligences. Following this view, a great athlete, an outstanding musician, or a creative writer each has high levels of different intelligences.

Despite the ongoing debate about definition, intelligence is usually defined by the test used to measure it. Most traditional intelligence tests emphasize one general intelligence that includes logic, spatial, and verbal abilities.

In 1904 the French school system commissioned Alfred Binet and Théodore Simon to identify "dull" students who would not benefit from school. Binet and Simon developed a test that contained items that measured different cognitive processes, such as attention, memory, and reasoning. The tests successfully distinguished respective students' abilities to respond to questions that measured these processes, and a new era was born.

Lewis Terman, who worked at Stanford University at about this time, brought the tests to the United States, and they were soon renamed the Stanford-Binet tests. Test items were ranked by difficulty, so there were items most 6-year-olds

Saying "That's So Retarded" is So Hurtful!

In the past, the term **mental retardation** referred to a generalized disability characterized by slower learning and development. The term is no longer used as a diagnosis, in part because it has turned into a derogatory term. "You're so retarded" and "That's retarded" are phrases commonly used to insult or degrade. When individuals diagnosed with mental retardation or friends and family of individuals with mental retardation heard such expressions, they were justifiably hurt, upset, and offended. The phrase was perceived as so offensive and potentially damaging that in 2006, members of the advocacy and support group the *American Association on Mental Retardation* voted to change their name to the *American Association on Intellectual and Developmental Disabilities*.

An intellectual disability is a type of developmental disability. A **developmental disability** is an umbrella classification for a diverse group of lifelong conditions resulting from mental or physical impairments. An **intellectual disability** is characterized by mental delays. Cognitive skills are significantly below average, showing delays in learning, reasoning, and problem solving. Diagnosis requires an IQ of less than 70, observable difficulties with activities of daily living, and symptoms that begin before age 18. Compared to children with average IQ, children with an intellectual disability require more repetition to learn and have difficulty generalizing what they learn in one situation to other situations. However, they can and do learn.

Intellectual delays are global and impact language development, social skills, and personal care. Activities of daily living, such as dressing alone, feeding one's self, communicating with others, and having a general understanding of things

could answer, items most 7-year-olds could answer, and so on. Mental age (MA) was determined by the most difficult type of items a child could respond to correctly. Scores were reported using an **intelligence quotient (IQ)**. With this scoring system, a child's mental age was divided by chronological age (CA) and multiplied by 100 (MA/CA x 100). So a 10-year-old child who succeed on items that most 10-year-olds could handle had an IQ of 100 (10/10 x 100). But if the 10-year-old was able to complete items only up to the 8-year-old level, that 10-year-old would have an IQ of 80. IQ tests are no longer scored this way, but it is helpful to understand the original meaning and methodology behind the numbers.

As children get older their mental age increases. When mental age and chronological age increase at the same rate, IQ stays the same. Research shows IQ scores stay relatively stable when there are short intervals between tests. For some individuals however scores go up and/or down, and fluctuations appear to be related to changes in life situation—disadvantaged environments lead to drops, and stimulating and supportive environments lead to gains.

that are happening in one's environment, are skills necessary for living independently (or as independently as appropriate for one's age).

The final criterion for diagnosis is age of onset (i.e., symptoms must appear before age 18). Most individuals with an intellectual disability or developmental delay are diagnosed in early childhood. Diagnoses tend to be earlier in cases with more significant delays. In some individuals, however, onset will come later. For example, if a child is exposed to dust from lead paint, he might start off life with no disability, but after the exposure to lead dust have brain damage, and be diagnosed with an intellectual disability. In contrast, because intellectual development is presumed to be complete by age 18, brain damage that occurs after 18-years of age would be considered traumatic brain injury rather than developmental delay.

With intellectual disabilities, degree of disability can vary tremendously. As adults, some individuals will need minimal support and be able to work and live independently, some may require more support and live with parents or in a group home, and others will be unable to work or even communicate effectively and will require daily and lifelong supervision. The degree of disability is often linked to its cause.

There are many causes of an intellectual disability. Some arise during the prenatal period; others arise after birth. All involve insult to the brain. Potential causes include exposure to environmental hazards (such as lead or drugs); brain damage from trauma (such as being shaken); chromosomal abnormalities (such as Down's syndrome); or nutritional deprivation. About 75 percent of the time the sole explanation for the delay is an impoverished environment. Intellectual disability resulting from an impoverished environment is preventable, and early intervention has proven successful at improving functioning.

So is IQ due to nature (biology) or nurture (environment)? Studies of identical twins (twins with the same genetic make-up) and fraternal twins (twins with about half the same genes) indicate that IQ scores for identical twins show higher degrees of similarity than scores for fraternal twins do. Hence, those with identical genetics have more similar IQs than those with fewer common genes. It has also been found that twins raised in the same home have more similar IQ scores than those raised separately. It is thus apparent that both genetics and environment (nature and nurture) influence IQ.

Knowledge that the environment can influence IQ is important because this means that changing a poor environment could improve IQ. For example, when Charles Nelson and his colleagues studied Romanian orphans placed with trained foster parents, and orphans in state-run orphanages (see Chapter 3), they found those with foster families had on average 8 points higher IQ scores. Children placed with foster parents earlier had higher IQs, and children put in foster care after 2 years of age made lower gains. Both groups had lower IQs than a comparison group of children raised with their biological families.

Standardized Testing

Although using intelligence tests to study cognitive development is referred to as the "psychometric approach," in practice the work of psychometricians is much broader. Psychometricians work with tests of cognitive, personality, social, emotional, or behavioral abilities. So whether it is a licensing exam to enter a profession, an entrance exam for employment or admission to school, or a screening inventory used by psychologists, it was probably developed with the assistance of psychometricians. Psychometricians insure that tests are accurate and fair—in large part this is achieved by standardization.

A standardized test is administered and scored the same for all test takers—in other words, the test is *standard* for all. When people think about standardized tests, they often imagine a big room filled with people using pencils to fill in bubbles in response to multiple choice or true-false questions. Some standardized tests, such as the SAT, are indeed administered to large groups, but some, such as the Strange Situation or the Stanford-Binet (currently in its fifth edition), are individually administered. Some require using a pencil to fill in bubbles, whereas others ask test-takers to show written work, produce a product, or type responses into a computer. The objective of standardization is fairness—everyone has the same experience. It would be neither fair nor standardized if some test takers had more time than others, if some took the test in a noisy room while others took it in a quiet room, or if some had their tests corrected by a hard grader while others had their tests corrected by an easy grader.

Some scores for tests are norm-referenced and others are criterion-referenced. Chapter 4 explained that *norms* involve looking at large numbers of individuals to see what is typical, or normal. **Norm-referenced tests** compare test takers to a **norm group**. But what constitutes the norm group? Other test takers who took the test that day? All test takers who have ever taken the test? The answer is neither. After test developers create a test, they administer it to a representative sample of people using the standard procedures. Test scores for this norm group are called norms. Every time the test is used, the scores are compared to those generated by the original norm group, and the scores reflect this comparison. So for example, the **percentile rank** is often reported for a score. A test taker who scored in the 95th percentile scored higher than 95 percent of the norm group. It is important that the norm group represent actual test takers. For example, if an 11-year-old girl took a test, and her score were compared back to a norm group of boys between 12 and 18 years of age, that score would be meaningless.

For **criterion-referenced tests** there is a criterion, or a collection of material the test is supposed to measure. For example, the criterion may be "students should correctly label parts of the brain." A group of experts decide what scores at different points on the scale mean. Most regular classroom tests written by teachers are criterion-referenced—the goal is to see if a student has learned a specific body of material.

Criterion-referenced tests show how test takers did compared to standards set by experts, and norm-referenced tests report how test takers performed compared to the norm group. Regardless of the type of test, however, it is important that great care go into ensuring tests are created, administered, scored, and interpreted in ways that are fair to all who take them. When students claim "I hate standardized tests!" it is doubtful that they truly hate standardization. Standardization is what makes the tests the same for everybody. The goal of standardization is to be fair.

Standards-Based Education Reform

In the United States, standardized tests have been in the spotlight because of federal laws. In 1994 legislation encouraged state governments to set high standards for all children. So states defined the content they wanted students to know and the standards students should meet. For the first time, schools had clear guidelines about what students were expected to learn. Standardized tests were used to see if these requisite standards were met.

In 2001 **No Child Left Behind** (NCLB) linked federal education money to school improvement. The goal was to ensure that every child, regardless of income, ethnicity, or background, achieved prescribed standards. This approach to improving education is called **standards based education reform.** NCLB required states to test students every year from third through eighth grade, and once in high school. States had to make test results public for all schools and were required to compile separate results for groups such as ethnic minorities (e.g., African American, Latino), students from low-income families, and students with disabilities. Gains for these different groups were evaluated, and schools could no longer "look good" if only the majority group performed well. One goal of NCLB was to close the **achievement gap**—the achievement differences found between students who are rich and poor, black and white, disabled and non-disabled. Debate continues as to whether or not the gap is closing. For most of the poorest schools, scores among minority children rose, but differences persist, and some schools have done a better job than others.

Critics of NCLB argue that all students should not be held to the same standards. They say standardized tests do not test important things, like creativity, and too much time is wasted "teaching to the test," leaving teachers little time to engage in more creative activities. In contrast, supporters of NCLB say yearly testing allows teachers and principals to regularly evaluate curriculum to see what works and doesn't work. Supporters also point out that teachers now have clear goals and that principals, parents, and the community can now see how schools are doing.

SCHOOLS AND THE CONTEXT OF LEARNING

Middle childhood is a time characterized by extensive learning, and schools have an enormous effect on cognitive development. Cultures around the world recognize this and although the quality of education varies tremendously, the majority of children around the world now attend at least some primary school.

Research suggests that many factors contribute to improving student learning and obtaining a high quality education. Involved and supportive families, exposure to early childhood education, smaller class sizes, teachers who are responsive to each child's learning needs, more hours in school, and a comprehensive educational philosophy each contribute to a better school experience.

The most consistent risk factor for school failure is poverty. Poor children often face a host of risk factors in addition to poverty. Residing in a crumbling home; attending school in a dilapidated building; lacking access to good health care and adequate nutrition; and living in a neighborhood filled with crime, violence, and drugs often go hand in hand with poverty. In the late 1990s Geoffrey Canada and the **Harlem Children's Zone** began an intervention project to improve life for youth in a 100-block area of Harlem, New York. Using public and private money, this locally run project provides an assortment of services.

Early intervention is the first component. There are parenting classes for parents of infants and toddlers, high-quality preschool programs, and extended-day charter elementary and high schools. A limited number of students can participate, so the project offers programs that are open to public school children, such as community-wide after-school programs; health clinics; and social services, including foster-care prevention programs.

Regular evaluation data are an important feature of the project. Teachers use test results to inform their teaching and evaluate the success of programs. Data show the achievement gap is closing rapidly within the Harlem Children's Zone; however, a gap still exists, and it is difficult to know which features of the program are most important to its success. However, an ecological perspective argues that the success lies in its comprehensive approach and that searching for the most important components is counterintuitive.

SOCIAL AND EMOTIONAL DEVELOPMENT

An ecological perspective is also helpful to understand social and emotional development. During middle childhood a child's social world increases. Schools, peers, and culture are all important components of this world; nonetheless, the center of the child's life is the family.

TABLE 5.1
Parenting Styles

	High Warmth	Low Warmth
High Control	Authoritative	Authoritarian
Low Control	Permissive Indulgent	Permissive Indifferent

Parents and Parenting Style

Parents have different beliefs and strategies for raising children. Researchers call this **parenting styles**. In the 1960s, psychologist Diana Baumrind studied 134 preschoolers from white upper-income families living in and around Berkeley, California. Observers coded child and parent behaviors during **naturalistic observation**—observations made in the regular environment. Baumrind wanted to describe parenting and determine whether parenting was related to child behaviors.

In her study, Baumrind identified four important dimensions of parenting: warmth, control, communication, and maturity demands. Using these dimensions, she presented three parenting styles: authoritative (high control, communication, and warmth), authoritarian (high control, low warmth and communication), and permissive (low control). She found authoritative parents were most likely to have socially responsible and independent children.

Since her original work, Baumrind and others have fine-tuned her initial conceptualizations. Today most researchers consider two important dimensions: warmth and control. These dimensions are dichotomized to delineate four parenting styles.

Permissive indulgent parents are warm, affectionate, communicative, and have few rules. Some lack rules because they want to avoid conflict. They are usually involved in the child's life, and sometimes are their child's friend. Longitudinal studies have found that children of permissive indulgent parents have lower academic performance, act less maturely, and can be aggressive.

Permissive indifferent parents are uninvolved and can be neglectful. They are unaware of what their child is doing, are cold, have few rules, engage in little communication, and show high maturity demands because children must care for themselves. Parents may be uninvolved because of work, an addiction, mental illness, or distance; regardless of the reason, they offer little to their children. Children with permissive indifferent parents tend to be less achievement oriented and lack self-control.

Authoritarian parents have high control and maturity demands, and low communication and warmth. Their parenting style can be reflected in two commonly used expressions: "It's my way or the highway" or "Children are to be seen and not heard." Research shows children of authoritarian parents tend to have lower academic performance and poorer social skills. They are often either out of control or overly controlled and subdued.

Authoritative parents have clear rules for children and consequences if rules are broken. They are communicative and flexible with rules, within reason. They also have realistic maturity demands and expect children to engage in age-appropriate self-care. Children of authoritative parents grow up to have higher academic performance and self-esteem, more independence, self-confidence, and altruism.

It appears that combining rules with warmth is the best strategy. A lack of warmth leads to aggression, and at least some control and discipline is important to ultimately teach children self-control.

But families are complex. Parenting styles can change; a parent may be authoritative to the hilt and then go through a difficult time and become permissive. Sometimes two parents in a single family have different parenting styles. In other instances, parents may use one parenting style with one child and a different style with that child's sibling. What is most important to children is the overall amount of warmth, discipline, and communication they are exposed to.

Culture and Parenting Styles

Baumrind's original research studied only white children, and this was the research trend for several decades. Today, research on parenting styles with non-white children is on the rise. Some of the research supports Baumrind's theory, and some suggests the meaning of various parenting styles depends on culture. For example, some parenting practices that are not authoritative also show benefits for children. For example, compared to Euro-American parents, Japanese parents generally use less control and more empathy and thus may appear permissive. In China many parents exert high control and less overt warmth, making them appear authoritarian; Latino parents on the other hand show warmth, but have high demands for respect for authority, which often makes them appear authoritarian. African American parents tend to show harsher discipline than parents of other cultures, but almost invariably couple this with reasoning and warmth.

What do these differences mean? For one thing, they demonstrate that the authoritative approach may not be the best parenting style for all groups and that cultural context is important to determine what is best. These differences all suggest that authoritative parenting is expressed differently in different cultures. Within the context of their own culture, for example, Japanese parents

Is It Authoritarian or Authoritative?

Students often struggle with the difference between the words authoritarian and authoritative. Breaking the words down can be helpful. Both have the root word *authority*. So both parenting styles expect children to obey and both have consequences if rules are broken. The suffix *–arian* can be found in words like veterinarian, vegetarian, and librarian. This suffix denotes "a strong commitment or obsession." Veterinarians are committed to animals, vegetarians are obsessed with vegetables, librarians are obsessed with books, and authoritarian parents have a strong commitment or obsession with authority.

In contrast, the suffix *–ative* means "tending to or inclined toward." This suffix can be seen in words such as relative (a tendency to relate), communicative (a tendency to communicate), and talkative (a tendency to talk), all demonstrating a leaning toward the root word. Authoritative parents lean toward authority, but are flexible and not obsessed with it.

classified as permissive by Western cultural norms may actually be authoritative. Clearly this topic requires more research.

Siblings

Sibling relationships can last longer than all other relationship and tend to be emotionally fraught. Siblings may be "best friends" or "worst enemies" or both. **Birth order**, the age position siblings hold in a family, is a popular topic of study. Usually birth order is ranked—oldest, middle, youngest, and only—and then the characteristics of people of the same birth order are explored. Birth order has been studied in relation to variables such as personality, social skills, intelligence, education, economic earnings, job selection, height, and weight. Because research on birth order has found mixed results, some say there is little scientific basis to the idea that birth order influences these variables; others contend there are clear differences. For example, research on personality has found slight differences, which suggest that firstborn children are more conscientious, organized, and diligent, whereas later-born children are more agreeable and less anxious. But these differences are very small and are not supported by every study.

The connection between birth order and intelligence has also been debated. Within large samples, there are slight but consistent differences. Petter Kristensen and Tor Bjerkendal studied 244,000 men drafted into the Norweigen army and found the average IQ of firstborn men was about 3 points higher than the IQ of second-born men, who had about 1 point advantage over later-born men.

Economist Sandra Black and colleagues also found older siblings made about 1 percent more money than their younger siblings did. Many theories attempt to explain these minor differences, ranging from better rest and nutrition during first pregnancies to more financial and emotional resources available for firstborns.

Although it is a topic of interest in popular culture, birth-order research is often criticized because it is difficult to design well-controlled studies. Families are structured in so many ways, it is sometimes tricky to label birth order; factors like family size, the presence of half-siblings and step-siblings, siblings with large age differences, and sibling gender make it difficult to conduct and replicate studies.

Family Functioning and Structure

Children have many needs. Some are concrete (like food, clothing, shelter, and safety); others are less tangible (like affection, praise, guidance, encouragement, stability, and peace). **Family functioning** refers to how well a family meets

Child Maltreatment and the Cycle of Violence

Child maltreatment is any non-accidental physical or psychological injury to a child, including physical abuse, sexual abuse, emotional abuse, and neglect. Child neglect occurs when guardians do not provide for the physical or emotional needs of the child, such as food, clothing, shelter, medical attention, safety, or supervision.

Child maltreatment does not discriminate—it occurs at every socioeconomic and education level, in every ethnic and cultural group, in every religion, and occurs about equally to boys and girls, although girls suffer higher rates of sexual abuse, whereas boys suffer higher rates of physical abuse.

Accurate rates of maltreatment are impossible to determine, but the U.S. Department of Health and Human Services estimates that almost 6 million children are involved in child abuse reports every year, and about five children a day die from child abuse. Often children do not disclose victimization. Each child responds differently. Child symptoms of maltreatment include the following:

- *Physical abuse*: broken bones; burns; welts; head injuries; bruises; the child is fearful or withdrawn, has unusual injuries, such as bruises on the thighs, ears, or stomach.

- *Emotional abuse*: poor social skills; emotional delays; speech disorders; cognitive delays; sleep problems; aggressiveness.

the needs of its members. **Family structure** refers to the legal, biological, and practical relationships between and among family members. Families can be structured in many ways: single-parent or two-parents; adoptive parents; foster parents; married, never-married, widowed or divorced parents; heterosexual, lesbian or gay parents; step-parents; grandparents who parent; teen or older parents; one child, or many children . . . the list goes on and on.

For many years researchers studied families by comparing **nuclear families** of heterosexual married parents and biological children to other family types, such as single-mother households. These comparisons almost always made the nuclear family look best. These families were more likely to have children who had friends, graduated high school, gained employment, were well adjusted, and were not depressed, anxious, or angry. But not all nuclear families work well. More recently, social scientists have come to understand the reason the average nuclear family looked best is because it is more likely to provide for children's needs and function effectively.

- *Sexual Abuse*: difficulty walking; genital pain, itching, or bleeding; urinary or yeast infections; sexually transmitted infections; complaints about stomachaches or headaches; fear of physical contact; inappropriate sexual knowledge.

- *Neglect*: chronically dirty, hungry, or inappropriately dressed; lack dental or medical attention; poor school attendance; unsupervised; self-destructive; substance abuse.

Long-term consequences depend on type of maltreatment, its frequency, relationship to perpetrator, and whether or not the child has talked to a supportive person. Child victims can grow up to have higher rates of relationship problems; mental illness, such as depression; alcohol or substance abuse; and crime.

Perpetrators of maltreatment are diverse with respect to racial background, religion, education, marital status, and income. Gay and lesbian adults are less likely to sexually abuse children than heterosexual adults, according to research by psychologists. About 30 percent of abused and neglected children will later abuse their own children. This is called the **cycle of abuse**. But not all victims become perpetrators—most in fact do not.

Breaking the cycle of violence is possible. Intervention is important. Intervention close to the time of abuse is best, but dealing with maltreatment during adulthood is also beneficial. Whether it involves talking to a loved one or a therapist, talking about and acknowledging what happened is important. Trying not to think about it usually means adults repeat patterns of abuse toward self or others.

Revisiting Gerard

I was going to Spain. The day I dreaded had finally come. I had been trying to convince my parents to let me live with my friend for the six months they would be in Spain. Of course it didn't work. I watched a movie on the eight-hour flight I had dreaded.

When we got to Spain we checked into our hotel. When we got to our room we found a beach ball in our suitcase from our last trip. We played soccer in our room with the beach ball. We played if you get it under the bed it's a goal. We stayed up until one o'clock in the morning but since we were still on American time, it felt like seven o'clock in the night. We didn't have breakfast because we woke up at ten in the morning. We had been invited to a friend's house. We were driven there. When we got there it was so fun! My favorite game we played was basketball. Patrick and I played against my dad and Jose Lewis. Patrick and I won. A few days later we moved into an apartment. I got to sleep on the trundle bed.

Some parts of Spain were good and some were bad. Everything was completely different. School was most different because you do nothing like at home. Spain school is better because it's shorter, that's what I say.

Today social scientists know family functioning is more important than family structure. A stable, loving, supportive, safe, harmonious household will produce children who do well regardless of whether parents are married or unmarried, gay or straight, adoptive or biological. Scientists must now figure out how to help families optimize family functioning.

CONCLUSION

Compared to early childhood, physical growth during middle childhood is slow and steady. Changes in the brain are linked to advances in cognitive development. Children in Piaget's concrete operational stage are more logical and can more effectively attend and remember. Individual differences in cognitive abilities can be measured by standardized tests. Educating children is a complex endeavor, and there are many levels of influence on individual children, with family playing a vital role. Warm and involved parents who also have rules and discipline in the household provide families that function best.

Further Reading

Jenny, C., T.A. Roesler, and K.L. Poyer. "Are Children at Risk for Sexual Abuse by Homosexuals?" *Pediatrics* 94, no. 1 (1994): 41–44.

Kirn, Walter. "Should You Stay Together for the Kids?" *Time* (November 6, 2000). Accessed August 1, 2011; available from http://www.time.com/time/world/article/0,8599,2056159,00.html#ixzz1UYILlT00

National Institute of Child Health and Human Development. Available at http://www .nichd.nih.gov/

Saxe, G.B. "The Mathematics of Child Street Vendors." *Child Development* 59 (1988): 1415–1425.

Society for Research in Child Development. Available at http://www.srcd.org/

The Harlem Children's Zome: http://www.hcz.org

Tyre, Peg. "A's for Good Behavior." *The New York Times* (November 27, 2010). Accessed August 1, 2011; available from http://www.nytimes.com/2010/11/28/weekinreview/28tyre.html?sq=Standards%20Based%20Education&st=cse&adxnnl=1&scp=1&adxnnlx=1312908599-5cKEHy0EDQycuUV1aosLbA

U.S. Department of Health & Human Services, Administration on Children Youth & Families. *Child Maltreatment 2007.* Washington, DC: U.S. Government Printing Office, 2009. Retrieved July 21, 2010, from http://www.acf.hhs.gov/programs/cb/pubs/cm07/index.htm

CHAPTER 6

DEVELOPMENT DURING ADOLESCENCE AND YOUNG ADULTHOOD

AGE THIRTEEN TO AGE TWENTY-FIVE

The words "adolescent" and "adult" both come from the same Latin word, *adolēscere*, which means "to grow up." *Adolescent* applies to someone who is growing up; adult applies to someone already grown up. Adolescence as a life stage is the bridge between childhood and before adulthood. It is clearly a time of growing up, when it begins and when it ends is not always as clear.

There are many ways to determine the beginning or end of a life phase. There are legal demarcations, such as laws that regulate things like drinking alcohol, voting, driving; and physical demarcations, such as puberty or menopause. Cognitive markers include the acquisition of concrete or abstract thought, and changes in social status (such as graduation, financial independence, marriage, or widowhood) can also serve as beginning or end points of particular life phases.

Most commonly it is puberty that denotes the beginning of adolescence, with a change in social status marking the end. In some cultures (mostly in the West), financial independence is the prevalent social status change that signals the end of adolescence; other status changes (common in many cultures) include marriage or military service. This definition of adolescence can be confusing because age for the beginning and end points is not fixed but can vary tremendously from individual to individual. For one person, puberty may begin at age 8; for another, it may not begin until age 16. Some young people move out of the parental home and marry at age 16; others remain dependent on their parents and live in their home into their mid-20s (or even later). The sidebar accompanying this discussion illustrates just how difficult it is to pinpoint the beginning and end of adolescence. The sidebar concerns two siblings but is told from the perspective of the sister, who tells us quite a bit about herself, her brother, her parents, and other people in her life. Suzette is a mother, but is she an adult? At the age of 17, David supported himself, his mother, and his sister. Was he an adult?

Obviously, the issues confronting 13- and 14-year-olds are very different from issues that a 21 or 25-year-old struggles with. For the latter group in

Suzette and David

Hey everybody. I'm Suzette. I hardly ever talk about my family. I don't know how I feel about my parents or anything, like who I am, and what to do with my life. I am 18, and have a son who is 2. We live with my grandparents who help me out.

My parents divorced a while ago. I don't think they wanted to marry, but they were dating and marriage was the thing to do. They fought every night. But, me and my brother still thought they would stay together. When I was 13 my mom wanted to divorce my dad. When she told me, I was relieved because my dad was very critical of me.

David, my brother, is 2 years older than me. We cried when we found out. My parents kept telling us they didn't want things to get ugly. I believed them, until my mom, told me she hated my dad. No matter how hard you try to stay out of it, you have to pick a side. At first I picked Mom's side, and David picked Dad's. When Dad moved out, David saw him but I didn't. It seemed like my dad was only there for my brother, not me.

My mom started to drink. We had to grow up fast. David worked and gave Mom money. I hardly saw him. But then Mom remarried. At first she didn't want us at the wedding, but we went. My stepfather isn't even close to a real father. I don't think their marriage will last. He is weird and flirts. Ever since sixth grade I looked grown-up and men flirt with me. It's disgusting.

I think I take my frustration out by seeking boyfriends. I guess I look for "love" in guys. Sometimes I do things sexually without really caring. But then, it makes a breakup harder. I got pregnant when I was 15. My boyfriend just left. My dad stopped talking to me. I had to move out from my mom's. We have no contact. I get depressed if I think about it.

I live with my grandparents. They help me and my son. I owe them a lot. I am also close to my brother. We talk to each other. I hope I will be a good mom, but I don't know. It's so hard since I don't even feel grown up myself.

particular, the terms adolescent and adolescence may seem a little strange—these terms seem to apply better to the younger end of the range. Acknowledging this, developmentalists also recognize a life period between adolescence and adulthood. This period generally begins around age 19 and lasts until the age of 25 or so. It is called **youth, young adulthood, early adulthood,** or **emerging adulthood.**

Regardless of exactly when adolescence begins and ends, it is a time of great change. The child is no longer a child. He or she is now capable of sexual reproduction, able to think abstractly as well as concretely, and able to survive independently. All of these changes raise challenges and can bring considerable angst.

HISTORICAL PERSPECTIVES OF ADOLESCENCE

Adolescence as a distinct life-stage did not exist for most of history. After sexual maturity individuals were adults. In 1904 G. Stanley Hall wrote the first book about adolescence as a distinct life stage. He described it as a time to prepare for adulthood and believed biology made adolescence a time of *Sturm und Drang* (literally *storm* and *stress* in German, the expression connotes turmoil).

In the late 1920s American anthropologist Margaret Mead used cross-cultural research to challenge Hall's ideas. She compared girls in the United States with Samoan girls who had a peaceful adolescence free from sexual restrictions and judgment. From this perspective, Mead posited that culture (nurture), not biology (nature), is what makes adolescence stressful. Thus began the debate about the relative influence of nature and nurture during adolescence.

During the 20th century, Western countries passed laws restricting child employment and requiring school attendance. This resulted in a dramatic increase in the number of high schools. The Great Depression and then World War II also changed the lives of adolescents. Military service enabled males to travel and interact with people very different from themselves, while females engaged in roles previously held exclusively by males. The end of World War II initiated the age of the **baby boomers,** a term referring to individuals born between 1946 and 1964. In the 1960s and 1970s, these baby boomers were adolescents, and marketers took note of their purchasing power. Unlike adults, adolescents had money to spend on non-essentials—music, clothing, entertainment, and fads like pet rocks[1] were marketed to teens. In many parts of the world today's adolescents continue to have a great deal of purchasing power, and companies continue to target them for non-essential and dispensable items.

---

[1] Pet rocks were gray stones sold in a box with "air holes." Around 1975, an estimated 5 million sold for $4 each.

Today's adolescents have access to life paths their parents did not have. Satellites and the Internet allow for almost instantaneous communication with others around the globe. Through various media, teens can see ways of life very different from their own. This rapid sharing of information has led to an increasingly common and widespread socialization known as **globalization**. Globalization is changing what teens around the world do. Sometimes the result is positive, such as the recent increase in knowledge about the dangers of female genital mutilation. But globalization also has a downside. One example is that it causes unique cultural practices to disappear, a phenomenon that has led to a decline in ceremonies that celebrate the life stage when young people reach adulthood.

PHYSICAL GROWTH AND DEVELOPMENT
Puberty
The impetus for most physical changes during adolescence is **puberty**. Puberty is a gradual process that begins years before any outward signs. It is responsible for a growth spurt in height and weight, changes in fat and muscle, changes in the circulatory and respiratory systems, and hormonal changes that cause the development of primary and secondary sex characteristics.

Scientists are unsure what makes puberty begin, but genetics, nutrition, and overall health play a role. Most evidence points to **leptin**, a protein produced by fat cells, as the trigger for puberty. This is why on average heavier adolescents and adolescents from rich countries enter puberty earlier, whereas later puberty is associated with malnutrition, excessive exercise, eating disorders, and illnesses. One prerequisite for the onset of puberty is that the individual's body fat must be approximately 19 percent of total body composition. From an evolutionary perspective, the need for body fat for reproduction makes sense. An adolescent with very low body fat probably lives in an environment that could not sustain a baby, so nature prudently keeps the body infertile.

Puberty is controlled by a **feedback loop** between the hypothalamus (a small part of the brain just above the brain stem), the pituitary gland (often called the master gland because it controls hormone levels in general), and the gonads (in females the ovaries, and in males the testes). The **hypothalamus** controls things like hunger, thirst, and sleep/wake cycles, and it also produces gonadotropin-releasing hormone (GnRH). GnRH stimulates the **pituitary gland** to produce hormones called gonadotropins. Gonadotropins stimulate the **gonads** to release the "sex" hormones, androgens and estrogens, into the bloodstream. Males and females both have estrogens and androgens (such as testosterone), but after puberty, males have proportionately more androgens and females have more estrogens. The sex hormones are responsible for sexual maturation and the other physical changes seen during puberty, such as breast development in females and facial hair growth in males. While all of this is happening, the

Fig. 6.1 Hypothalamus-Pituitary-Gonad Feedback Loop

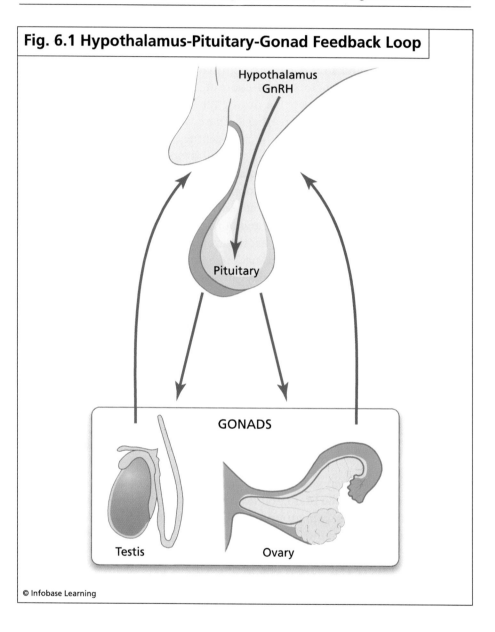

Hypothalamus
GnRH

Pituitary

GONADS

Testis

Ovary

© Infobase Learning

hypothalamus constantly monitors levels of androgens and estrogens in the bloodstream—when they fall too low, more GnRH is released; when they get too high, less GnRH is released. This balancing activity explains the concept of feedback loop.

On average, the first signs of puberty in girls occur at age 10½,; for boys they occur between 11½ and 12. But these numbers are averages, and variation among individuals is normal. One sign of puberty in girls is the first menstrual period, also called **menarche**. Today, menarche occurs on average at 12½, but any age between 9 and 15 is considered normal. For generations girls recorded this event in diaries, or doctors made a note of it in their charts. Historians can look at written records and see that during the 1800s most girls had their first period at approximately 17 years of age. There was a steady decline in age of menarche during the first part of the 20th century, but by the end of the 20th century, the average age of menarche stopped dropping. This decrease in age of first menstruation is called the **secular trend**, a historical trend indicating a change in body size or timing of development.

Many have speculated about the cause of this secular trend. Things like pollution, promiscuous cultural values, and hormones in foods have been blamed. But cross-cultural evidence shows that the average age of menarche varies from country to country. In industrialized nations where adolescents have easy access to good nutrition and spend their days in school or in front of an electronic screen, the average age of menarche is lower than in non-industrialized countries. When girls engage in hard physical labor and lack access to good nutrition, menarche is later. This suggests the main cause of the secular trend is changes in body fat, which is closely related to the onset of puberty.

THE NERVOUS SYSTEM AND BRAIN DEVELOPMENT

Recently, much attention has been paid to brain development during adolescence. In part, this is because new research techniques allow scientists to see the brain as it works; this trend has also been influenced because of an increased recognition of adolescence as a stage distinctly separate and different from adulthood.

During the first two years of life, there is a period of overproduction of neural connections in the brain, followed by a period of pruning unused connections. This happens again around the time of puberty. First there is a period of overproduction of synaptic connections in the outer layer of the brain. This overproduction peaks around the age of 11 or 12 and is especially concentrated in the **frontal lobe.** The frontal lobe is situated just behind the forehead. It is responsible for executive functions. Just like an executive in a company is the boss, the frontal lobe is the boss of the brain and has a many different responsibilities. It is in charge of solving problems, making decisions, directing movement, emotions, personality, language, memory, sexual behavior, and impulse control.

For the next several years, into the early 20s, synaptic pruning occurs. It is estimated that as much as 10 percent of the outer layer of the brain is pruned away. Recall that unused synapses are pruned, with the brain following a "use-it or lose-it" principle. At the same time, the remaining neural pathways become myelinated. Myelin makes electrical impulses (messages) travel faster. So, by the end of adolescence the remaining brain is specialized and more efficient; however, it is less flexible and does not adapt to new things as easily as the brain of a child does.

Another region of the brain that experiences growth during adolescence and young adulthood is the **cerebellum**, a part of the lower brain involved in things like movement. The cerebellum also appears to assist cognitive functions such as decision-making, mathematics, language, music, and social skills. Cerebellum development continues through the early 20s.

Because an adolescent's brain is not yet fully developed, many individuals in this life stage have difficulty handling emotions, making good decisions, and managing social situations. There is an abundance of statistical evidence to show adolescents are the age group most likely to engage in risky behaviors, such as dangerous driving, substance use, risky sex, and delinquency. Increasingly brain research is used in criminal cases to argue against treating teenagers and adults the same. The argument is that a teen's brain is a work in progress, with the underlying message that teens should not be given the same penalties as adults because they are not entirely capable of making responsible, adult choices. Taking this a step further, some challenge the wisdom of allowing 16-year-olds to drive cars, 18-year-olds to vote and/or enlist in the military, and 21-year-olds to drink alcohol. Because the brain does not reach its full adult potential until about age 25, it appears only rental-car companies have determined the correct age marker for adulthood—most rental car companies will not rent a car to individuals under age 25.

COGNITIVE DEVELOPMENT

At the same time the adolescent's body and brain are developing, there are dramatic changes in cognition. Around the world, cultures recognize adolescents are more capable than children when tackling complex intellectual problems. A Piagetian approach will highlight some of these changes.

Piaget's Formal Operational Thought

According to Piaget, the final stage of cognitive development is **formal operations**, which begins around the age of 12. The most striking feature of this stage is that adolescents are capable of thinking about abstract concepts. Unlike concrete thinkers who are capable of using logic, but are limited by reality and what they have experienced, formal thinkers can understand complex, abstract, and hypothetical things.

Consider, for example, how a concrete child might describe herself: "I am 8 years old and a girl. I like horses, but I do not like cats. I have an older brother, and we live with my mother and grandmother. My best friend is Maria, and we like to play soccer." These are specific and tangible aspects of her life. In contrast, a formal thinker would say, "I am a person with deep feelings, but

I share my feelings only with good friends. I am usually extroverted, but I can be introverted when I don't know people. I am a good student most of the time, but if I dislike a teacher I tend to be inattentive." Unlike the concrete thinker, the formal thinker uses vague and intangible expressions to describe herself.

As abstract thinking increases, language use changes. The adolescent enjoys word analogies, metaphors, and puns that would confuse the younger child. Simple examples easily show the difference. School-age children like jokes with a twist on words, when one word has two meanings: "Why did the lady throw the butter out the window? To see the butterfly." or "Why did she throw the clock out the window? To see time fly." These are concrete ideas, and the image of the double meaning is what makes the joke funny to children. In contrast, adolescents enjoy language in a more mature way, even appreciating the analogies and metaphors found in literature: "What's in a name? That which we call a rose by any other name would smell as sweet" (Shakespeare's *Romeo and Juliette*, II, ii, 1–2). This does not necessarily mean that adolescent's appreciation of abstract language is high brow; the language found in "Yo momma" jokes show that they enjoy plenty of low-brow humor as well ("Yo momma's so ugly she makes onions cry," "Yo momma's so old, when someone told her to act her age she died.") Both the high-brow literary references and the low-brow jokes are likely to be enjoyed by formal thinkers but are just as likely to be misunderstood or taken literally by concrete-thinking school-age children.

Formal thinkers also become more capable of focusing on the logic of verbal arguments. They develop the ability to hypothesize and to test and evaluate hypotheses. Piaget called this **hypothetical-deductive reasoning**, the process of considering what might affect the outcome of a problem and then systematically testing possibilities. Consider the following problem. "You are in a dark closet. There are 6 shoes of 3 colors, and 24 socks all of which are black or brown. How many socks and shoes must you take into the light to be sure you get a matching pair of socks and matching pair of shoes?" Using hypothetical-deductive reasoning, the formal thinker will pick one aspect of the problem first, such as socks, and systematically try different solutions. He or she will then address the second aspect of the problem in the same systematic manner. This process makes it easy to arrive at the correct answer.[2]

Formal thinkers can think about their thinking. **Metacognition** is the process of thinking about one's own cognitions, such as when one consciously repeats something over and over to remember it or uses a mnemonic such as "**M**y **v**ery **e**ager **m**other **j**ust **s**erved **u**s **n**ine-hundred **p**izzas" to help remember the order of the planets (the first letter of each word stands for a planet,

---

[2] To ensure you get a matching pair you need 3 socks and 4 shoes. With 2 colors of socks it doesn't matter how many are in the pile; if you take 3 socks, 2 will be the same color. Similarly, with 3 shoe colors you need to pick 4 shoes (selecting 3 could result in 1 shoe in each of color).

Mercury, Venus, Earth, Mars, etc.). Adolescents are also good at explaining their thoughts. If asked, "How did you solve that problem?" they can describe the steps they used to arrive at the solution.

Contemporary Views of Formal Operational Thought
Research shows that the transition to formal operations (like the transitions between other stages) is gradual and that an individual does not necessarily use formal operational thinking in all areas of life. For example, a child might use high level abstract thought when searching for clues and solving problems in a video game but think in a concrete manner when packing a backpack for school. Piaget did not recognize the real-life limitations of using logic all the time. Practical limitations, social situations, and emotions sometimes make the exclusive use of logic impractical.

Young Adults and Postformal Thought
According to Piaget, formal operations is the last stage of cognitive development. But contemporary research shows during young adulthood cognitive abilities continue to change. Psychologist Jan Sinnott calls the time after formal thought **postformal**. Unlike formal operations, postformal thought is pragmatic—contradictions in reality are expected, and there are no absolutes. **Pragmatism** involves consideration of real-life limitations in logical thinking. For example, although some people might be strongly opposed to abortion on moral grounds, they might also feel in some instances, such as when a mother's life is endangered, it is a valuable option. Rather than seeing an issue as black or white, right or wrong, the postformal thinker expects and accepts contradictions. Solutions are usually gray, not black or white. Postformal thinking often considers social and interpersonal variables when solving problems. This approach clearly recognizes the context of each individual problem and is viewed as a more mature approach to thinking.

SOCIAL COGNITION
Social cognition refers to how people think about the social world: other people, social situations, social institutions, and even the self. Most research suggests the development of social cognition can be explained using Piaget's stages. For example, the concrete thinker understands social situations in a concrete way. Recall the example earlier in this section in which the concrete thinker used global descriptions, such as age, gender, likes, and dislikes to describe herself. The adolescent described herself in more abstract terms, recognizing contradictions in herself and describing attitudes rather than physical attributes.

   With social cognition, adolescents also become better at taking the perspective of others. Whereas young children view their thoughts, interests, concerns, and experiences as being universal (e.g., Santa Claus comes to my house, so he must come to everybody's house), adolescents better understand that others might have experiences and thoughts different from their own. They are less egocentric—they can think about and imagine what others are thinking and feeling.

At the same time, young adolescents often take these new abilities to the extreme. Because their bodies and minds are going through so many changes, adolescents spend a great deal of time thinking about themselves. They also spend a lot of time thinking about how others see them. They believe others pay as much attention to their appearance as they themselves do. They feel like they are on a stage, and everyone is watching them. This feeling of constantly being watched is called the **imaginary audience.**

The imaginary audience makes teens very self-conscious. They believe everyone will notice a new haircut, or a pimple on the nose, or the fact that the same pants were worn twice in one week. Everyone will see if they make a mistake, and everyone will know if they somehow stood out or were different. Adults often see this as overreacting, but to adolescents it is very real. Wherever they go and whatever they do, they are being watched. Other age groups also have an imaginary audience, but the phenomenon is most prevalent during early adolescence.

Related to the imaginary audience is the **personal fable**, a phrase first used by David Elkind. Because adolescents feel watched all the time, they begin to believe "I must be special and unique." Over and over they tell themselves this personal fable: "I am unique. Nobody is like me." As a result, adolescents often feel alone and misunderstood. They holler at a parent, "You can't possibly understand what it feels like to be dumped. My love was deeper than any other love before." Or they use their own uniqueness to rationalize risky behavior, "I won't get drunk. I know how to hold my liquor." "I won't get in an accident, I drive better when speeding." "I won't get a sexually transmitted disease, I would never have sex with a sick person—I would know the difference." Eventually experience teaches most individuals they are not as unique as they thought, and the personal fable recedes.

The personal fable is an important concept to understand when trying to prevent or stop risky behaviors. But this begins with and understanding that adolescents believe in their uniqueness, which is one reason "scared straight" interventions usually fail. When a teen smoker sees a smoker's tar covered lung, he tells himself, "That won't happen to me, I am different, I can stop whenever I want." Or when misbehaving teenagers are walked through a high-security prison they think, "I am nothing like these criminals, I would never do what they did, and I would never get caught."

SOCIAL AND EMOTIONAL DEVELOPMENT

During adolescence young people must discover their sense of place in the world—their identity. Physically, they have the strength and body size of an

How Can You Stop Teens from Getting into Trouble?

Compared to children, most adolescents have greater physical abilities and more independence, so they can make decisions about their own behavior. Sometimes they engage in potentially dangerous or deadly **risk-taking** behaviors, such as substance use, violence or unsafe sex.

Prevention programs attempt to educate teens and stop risky behaviors from occurring. **Intervention programs** try to minimize consequences of behaviors that have already occurred. Developmentalists have designed programs to prevent or stop behaviors such as substance use, dropping out of school, depression, suicide, eating disorders, risky sexual behaviors, and aggressive behaviors related to driving, bullying, or violence. Some programs are more effective than others. Programs are more likely to fail when they attempt to scare or guilt teens into good behavior. More effective measures balance education about risk with positive youth development.

Generally, effective programs are **comprehensive**. A comprehensive program might teach students facts, problem solving and decision-making skills; they also help develop interpersonal skills. Because of the personal fable, those involved in running such programs avoid speaking in global terms. Rather than saying, "If you smoke cigarettes you will die of lung cancer in 40 years," they emphasize factors immediately relevant to the young person: "If you smoke, your breath and hair will smell and partners will not want to kiss you." In addition, developmentalists recognize that it is important to change the environment, for example, by making health centers accessible or by changing laws. And finally, they understand that effective programs last a long time, and are tailored to the specific levels of experience, ages, genders, sexual orientation, and economic or cultural background of participants.

adult, can take on adult work, and can sexually reproduce, so they can consider career, sexuality, and partnering options. Cognitively they can think about their own strengths and weaknesses and determine what life paths they might follow. And socially, they are expected to know what they want to do with their lives (graduating seniors are constantly asked, "What are you doing next year?"). Earlier in this chapter, you read the musings of an adolescent named Suzette, which illustrated this desire to figure out a sense of self. Erik Erikson called this struggle the **identity crisis**.

Identity

Erik Erikson's personality theory of eight psychosocial stages describes adolescence as the time to answer three questions: Who am I? Where am I going? Who am I to become? He called the adolescent's struggle to answer these questions an identity crisis. During this transition from childhood to adulthood, adolescents have numerous choices. They must decide upon a vocation; acquire a philosophy of life (e.g., political beliefs); adopt a system of values (e.g., religious and moral values); and adopt a set of social roles (e.g., sex roles). Additionally, past roles must be incorporated into the newly emerging sense of self and with ideas about the future self. For example, the 17-year-old must incorporate her former "straight-A-student" self into her current "party-animal" self and must also combine these factors to form what she hopes is her future "successful-lawyer" self.

Research on identity supports Erikson's main ideas; however, his time frame has been challenged. Erikson believed the identity crisis happened during adolescence, and identity issues could resurface at other life stages. Contemporary psychologists agree that identity issues can reemerge, but they place identity development in early adulthood.

James Marcia is a contemporary psychologist who expanded on Erikson's ideas. He emphasized two aspects of the identity crisis, **exploration** (crisis) and **commitment**. Exploration involves questioning the "self," choosing basic moral beliefs, interpersonal styles, habits, and life goals. Commitment is the extent to which there is a personal investment in roles and beliefs. Exploration and commitment involve experimenting with different roles and personalities before eventually resolving the identity crisis.

Marcia assigns people into one of four categories based on exploration and commitment. Individuals who are in the process of exploring but have not made commitments are in *moratorium*. For example, a college student who is thinking about different majors, has different groups of friends, and is considering different political positions, but has not yet made up his mind about any of these issues. The *foreclosed* individual has made commitments, but without a crisis. For example, she knows she wants to be a teacher and is a Democrat. She has always known this, never questioned it, and it is what family and friends expect. An individual with a *diffused* identity has not made commitments and is not exploring. He does not know how he fits into the world, does not worry about it, and is annoyed if challenged. "Why do I have to decide? Why can't I just live my life?" And finally, the *identity-achieved* individual has made commitments after a period of crisis and exploration. This individual knows who she is and what she believes, but she also understands many viewpoints because she considered those views while in moratorium.

How young people handle the identity crisis depends on several factors, including cognitive level, whether there are opportunities to explore, role models, and the role options available. Some parts of the world offer limited role options—individuals cannot select their own education, job, or even spouse. In these cultures, a foreclosed identity works well. In Western cultures, many role

TABLE 6.1
Marcia's Identity Statuses

		Exploration	
		Absent	Present
Commitment	Absent	Diffused	Moratorium
	Present	Foreclosed	Achieved

options exist; young people must decide their own academic and career paths, and select their own marriage partners. Under these circumstances, identity achieved is the goal; however, a moratorium must come first. It is common for adolescents in these cultures to explore.

Social Relationships
Adolescents have relationships with many people: parents, teachers, coaches, grandparents, siblings, friends, classmates, girlfriends, boyfriends, and bosses. In each relationship the adolescent has different roles and responsibilities.

Parents and Adolescents
Research by psychologist Reed Larson and colleagues in the United States shows that adolescents spend less time with family and more time alone or with friends than they did in childhood. They are also more likely to argue with parents. Nonetheless, most adolescents feel loved by and close to their parents.

According to psychologist Judith Smetana, one reason parents and teens argue is that they view issues from different perspectives. Young people feel parents fail to provide enough emotional support, and parents feel teens do not meet reasonable expectations. For example, when parents ask their daughter to clean her bedroom, the teenager's position is, "It's my room, I should be allowed to keep it the way I want." In contrast, her parents feel, "A family rule is to keep rooms neat. A messy bedroom shows disrespect for household standards." Similarly, when a teen wants a tattoo, he believes, "My parents should support my decisions about my body," whereas his parents feel, "We are still in charge. What our son does to his body reflects on the family."

Although some conflict is inevitable, a high degree of conflict is problematic. Parenting research shows adolescents want to be accepted by parents and make them proud. Parents who criticize, are harsh, lack warmth, or are overly

What Are You: Gay or Straight?

For most adolescents, the question "What are you?" does not bring to mind one's sexual orientation. However, adolescence is the main time individuals consider issues of identity, intimacy, and sexuality. So for adolescents who are gay, lesbian, bisexual or transgender (GLBT), sexual confusion and anxiety can be high, and the issue of sexuality is an important aspect of identity.

There are many terms that describe aspects of one's sexual orientation. **Homosexuality** applies to an individual who is sexually attracted to others of the same sex. Sometimes **gay** means the same as homosexual, but it is generally used to refer to males who are attracted to males. **Lesbian** refers only to females who are attracted to females. **Heterosexuality** applies to individuals who are sexually attracted to members of the opposite sex. **Bi-sexuality** refers to sexual attraction to both males and females. **Transgender** is a term that has an evolving definition—it usually refers to individuals who are labeled one sex at birth (male or female) but feel as if they are truly the opposite sex.

Western cultures presume that individuals are heterosexual, and socialization from parents, friends, school and the media all support this assumption. Until recently, images of dating, love and sexuality in the media were exclusively heterosexual. In adolescent relationships, males are generally expected to have "a girlfriend," and females are expected to have "a boyfriend."

Research shows that adolescence is the life stage during which most GLBT people become aware of their sexuality. This is part of coming-out. **Coming-**

strict (authoritarian parents) have children who feel bad about themselves. Parents who exert reasonable control, high levels of warmth and support, and have realistic maturity demands (authoritative parents) are more likely to have well-adjusted adolescents.

Teachers and Adolescents

Teachers undoubtedly have an impact on students. They impart knowledge, but they also affect students' social and emotional development.

In the late 1960s, researchers Robert Rosenthal and Lenore Jacobsen hypothesized that some students performed poorly in school because teachers expected them to. To test this hypothesis, they went into an elementary school and gave all students an intelligence test (the pre-test). Teachers were told the test predicted academic "blooming." In September, at the beginning of the school year, they were given the names of students with scores indicating faster learning abilities (the experimental group). All students took the test again

out, or coming-out-of-the-closet, refers to the steps taken to tell others about one's **sexual orientation** or **gender identity**. The process can be difficult, and reactions to self-recognition can range from happiness and relief, to anxiety and depression. Because coming-out is a process, adolescents often go through a stage when they tell themselves, "It's just a phase. I'll grow out of it."

Research by Richard Savin-Williams found that most adolescents come-out to a friend first, not to parents. Mothers are usually told before fathers, and mothers are more likely to suspect their child's sexual orientation before fathers do. The reactions of those told are important. Young people who get negative reactions are more likely to return to the closet, and **pass**–pretend to be straight.

Most GLBT teens report that they have been harassed, physically abused, or verbally abused by adults (including parents and teachers) and/or peers. So it is not surprising they have higher rates of suicide, substance abuse, running away, and school difficulties.

After 35 years of objective, well-designed, scientific research, it has been determined that homosexuality is neither an illness (mental or otherwise) nor an emotional problem. It does not require treatment nor is it changeable. Recently, some groups have offered "Conversion Therapy" to young people, with the goal of "converting" them to heterosexuality. Research on these therapies shows no scientific validity to the claim that individuals can be "converted," and the American Psychological Association has expressed serious concerns that such therapies are harmful.

mid-way through the school year, at the end of the school year, and 20 months later, after a year with a new teacher.

The experimental group of bloomers was compared to the unnamed students (the control group) and on average made greater gains. But the "bloomers" were actually randomly selected and scored no differently on the original test than the control group. The researchers attributed the bloomers' gains on the later tests to **self-fulfilling prophecy**—when others expect an individual to perform a particular way, that individual will live up to those expectations. Without realizing it, teachers had sent subtle cues about their expectations and the bloomers had responded by meeting those expectations.

Today this phenomenon has several names besides **self-fulfilling prophecy**; it is sometimes called the **Rosenthal effect** (because it confirms Rosenthal's hypothesis), **expectancy effects** (reflecting the behavior that expectations promote), or the **Pygmalion effect** (named after the Greek god who created a statue that was his personal vision of the perfect woman and fell in love with it).

Diagnoses and Labels:
What Does It Mean to Be Learning Disabled?

Many parents of children with disabilities fear their children will be treated differently from other children if they are diagnosed or labeled, a fear that reflects the principle of self-fulfilling prophecy. For example, in cases when a child has a **learning disability** (LD) some parents fear teachers will think their child is incapable of learning and won't spend as much time teaching their child as they might spend with other children. Alternatively, parents worry that children with learning disabilities will expect less of themselves and not try as hard as they would if they did not have the label.

The diagnosis of LD is given when there is a difference between a student's academic performance and potential. Children with LDs usually have average or above average intelligence, but perform below their age level in a specific academic area or areas, such as reading, writing, listening, speaking, reasoning, or mathematics.* For a diagnosis to be valid, the deficit must not be the result of inadequate education or caused by a physical disability such as vision or hearing impairment. Students with LDs usually work hard in school and are neither lazy nor dumb. Research has shown that their brains process information differently. There are probably multiple causes for this, including genetics and prenatal or postnatal exposure to trauma or toxins. Although a LD is a lifelong condition, students can be taught ways to work around their disability and process information in a way that allows them to succeed in school.

Today's laws prohibit discrimination based on a disability and require schools to provide special education to children with disabilities, including LDs. Nonetheless, students diagnosed with a LD may still experience discrimination—teachers may treat them differently (sometimes unwittingly), schools and employers may be unwilling to make accommodations, and peers may tease or ridicule them.

It is important to note that there are potential benefits to the LD label. First of all, a diagnosis is a source of information. When a student learns that her difficulties are not caused by "laziness" or "stupidity," she is likely to experience tremendous relief. Secondly, a correct diagnosis can lead to appropriate remediation. A third benefit is economic as neither insurance companies nor school systems will pay for treatment until a student has been officially diagnosed. So parents and their children must balance the risks and benefits of labeling and decide what works best for them.

---

* An LD is different from an intellectual disability (formerly called mental retardation), which is a global disability affecting cognitive and social development.

Variations of Rosenthal's original studies have consistently found self-fulfilling prophecies do occur in the classroom, even though the effects are usually minimal. Furthermore, the effects also occur in other relationships, such as those between doctor and patient, therapist and client, experimenter and study participant, coach and athlete, manager and employee, and judge and jury.

Friends and Peers

Adolescents spend less time with family and more time with peers, especially friends. **Peers** are individuals of the same age who share the same situational settings. So a classroom of students is a group of peers, as is a team of athletes. Peers may or may not have close relationships with each other. In contrast, a **friendship** is a mutual relationship that is valued by both partners.

Young children usually select friends based on convenience—that is, children who are nearby. School-age children form friendships based on shared activities and common interests, such as a pair of classmates who both love Harry Potter books. Adolescents are even more selective—a friend is someone to share and talk with, someone with common interests and values. Some teens also select friends to boost social status. Most turn to friends for understanding, support and guidance.

Friends are important. Adolescents without friends are more likely to be lonely, unhappy, have less academic success, and lower self-esteem. They are also more likely to engage in delinquent behavior and drop out of school. Social-skills training that teaches children to listen, converse, compliment, show humor, and manage strong emotions have shown some success at helping children make friends.

Peer pressure describes what happens when members of a peer group encourage a person to engage in a certain behavior or change a belief to demonstrate agreement and solidarity with the group. Sometimes it is overt: "If you don't smoke this cigarette, I won't be your friend." In most cases, however, the pressure is subtle: "We'll all be smoking together, why don't you join us?" Some researchers call this phenomenon **peer** or **friend's influence** rather than peer pressure. This influence can be either positive or negative. There can be pressure to engage in unhealthy or dangerous behaviors, such as smoking, drinking, or unprotected sex. On the other hand, there can be pressure to get good grades, avoid drugs, and exercise. Peers can influence major decisions (such as when to have sex) or minor decisions (such as choice of music or fashion).

CONCLUSION

Dramatic physical, emotional, and mental changes occur during adolescence and young adulthood. Many biological changes occur within a short period of time; as the brain changes, young people become increasingly capable of abstract and critical thinking. Social cognition also changes and adolescents and youth become better equipped to think about social situations. As a result of these changes, adolescents and young adults develop their own personal identities. Because adolescents spend time with so many different kinds of people (parents, teachers, peers), they are shaped by many different kinds of socialization.

Further Reading

Boerner, Leigh Krietsch. "First Period Tied to Girls' Weight." *Reuters* (March 17, 2011) accessed August 1, 2011; available from http://www.reuters.com/article/2011/03/17/us-first-period-tied-girl-weight-idUSTRE72G82J20110317

Drummond, Katie. "CDC: Kids Aren't Learning About Contraceptives in Sex Ed" *AOLNews*. (September 15, 2010) accessed August 1, 2011; available from http://www.aolnews.com/2010/09/15/cdc-kids-arent-learning-about-contraceptives-in-sex-ed/

Erikson, E. *Identity: youth and crisis.* Oxford England: Norton & Co., 1968.

Hoffman, Jan. "Fighting Teenage Pregnancy With MTV Stars as Exhibit A." *The New York Times* (April 8, 2011).

Savin-Williams, R.C. *Mom, Dad. I'm gay. How families negotiate coming out.* Washington DC: American Psychological Association, 2001.

Sinnott, J.D. *The Development of Logic in Adulthood: Postformal Thought and Its Applications.* New York, N.Y.: Plenum Press, 1998.

Society for Research on Adolescence. Available at http://www.s-r-a.org/

CHAPTER 7

DEVELOPMENT DURING ADULTHOOD

Adulthood lasts a long time and has many permutations. Many issues affect each distinct stage of adulthood but not in the same way. Other issues tend be specific to a particular stage of adulthood, such as early, middle, or later adulthood. The chapter describes physical development and how lifestyle habits can prevent or slow down physical decline. It also presents theories about intelligence during adulthood, a discussion on the complexity of social and emotional development, and a discussion of the numerous roles adults engage in. And because this book covers the entire lifespan, the chapter concludes with a discussion of death and dying.

Adulthood begins after adolescence and lasts until the end of life. For most, this is a very long time. Developmentalists recognize that just as in earlier life stages, physical, cognitive, social, and emotional development continues throughout the lifespan; however, unlike in earlier ages, changes during adulthood tend to be more gradual. Hence, adulthood is divided into three stages: early, middle, and late adulthood.

Early adulthood begins in the 20s and lasts through the 30s. Zenón is in early adulthood. He has recently moved from his childhood home and is just starting a career in a new city. He hopes to find a partner and start a family. Middle adulthood lasts from about 40 to 65. Both Gregoria and Tomas are in middle adulthood. They have noticed a decline in strength and physical abilities. They are responsible for a child and parent. Late adulthood begins at 65 and

Tomas and Gregoria

Tomas Domínguez Cri, age 47, and Gregoria Lupe Siles, age 46, live and farm in the Colomi municipality of Bolivia. They have been married 24 years. Tomas' 68-year-old mother Armanda and 16-year-old daughter Aureilam live with them. Their 21-year-old son, Zenón is a machine mechanic in La Paz. Tomas attended school for 2 years, but Gregoria and Armanda are illiterate. Gregoria says, "Everything we did was so the children could go to school and not have the same life we did."

Until ten years ago the family lived in Ayopaya. When his father died, Tomas inherited the house and property, but because of poor schools and poor farming, he decided to move to the Colomi municipality. Tomas says, "We had to leave family behind. We try to return, but it is not enough."

Since the move, their luck has improved. The family has five heads of cattle for milk, and they grow potatoes and other vegetables to sell at market. Tomas and Gregoria constantly work. Tomas awakes early to milk the cows, and then puts them out to pasture so he can tend to farm chores. In the evening he milks the cows again. Tomas hopes to save money for a yoke team to help with plowing and planting. "I can not work as hard as I used to—I need help, but I do not want my children to farm. I want them to be professionals."

In the morning, Gregoria delivers milk to the homes of regular customers. When she gets home, it is time to prepare the family's mid-day meal. In the afternoon Armanda and Gregoria prepare yogurt or other products to sell at market. The two women enjoy each other's company. What the family produces on their farm serves both for their own nutrition and for their income. Gregoria says, "I used to dream of having a successful farm. Now we are successful, but the work is constant."

Armanda reflects on her current situation and says, "This is a good life. We are comfortable. I think about my old home and those I have lost, my husband, a daughter, sisters, and friends. Everything happens for a reason. I am supposed to be here to help my children. They need me, and I need them, so everything is good."

ends with death. Armanda is in late adulthood. She is a contributing member of the family and is proud of the life she has lived.

BODY GROWTH AND DEVELOPMENT

During childhood and adolescence the body develops and changes to reach its full adult potential. Adulthood marks the beginning of **biological aging,** biologically determined declines in the body's functioning. Some changes are observable, such as graying hair, wrinkles, and a change in the muscle-to-fat ratio. Others are noticeable mostly by those experiencing them, such as changes in vision, the skeleton, reproductive system, and nervous system.

Physical Changes in Adulthood

Changes in physical appearance occur gradually during the 20s and 30s; however, beginning in the 30s, physical signs of aging become increasingly more apparent. Adulthood, for example, brings changes in vision. Beginning in the 40s most adults have difficulty seeing in dim light and focusing on close objects; many require glasses to read and drive. Around the age of 70 there is a sharp decline in visual acuity.

For many adults over 40 a larger waistline accompanies aging. Some call this the **middle-age spread**—excess weight accumulates around the abdomen and back in men and around the abdomen and upper arms in women. This fat is a major risk for cardiovascular disease and possibly some cancers. There are several causes of middle-age spread. The digestive system begins to break down and absorb nutrients from food less efficiently, and muscles and joints require more time to warm up. Also, beginning around age 40, muscle mass gradually declines, as does **basal metabolism,** the number of calories burned when the body is at rest. Fortunately, a decline in metabolism can be moderated by maintaining muscle mass. Muscle is one of the few tissues that can regenerate at any age; therefore, taking up exercise at any age is beneficial.

Many factors influence when the physical changes of adulthood occur. Genetics and lifestyle decisions, such as smoking, sun exposure, and diet can each play important roles.

Female Menopause

Around midlife, women experience dramatic biological changes associated with fertility. Just like puberty, **menopause** is a biological change that occurs over a period of years. It involves changing levels of hormones accompanied by changes in the reproductive system. The word menopause is derived from Greek words meaning the end of monthly cycles. The primary symptom is that the ovaries stop producing estradiol and progesterone, first resulting in less frequent periods, and ultimately resulting in the cessation of ovulation and menstruation. On average this occurs at age 51, but any time between 40 and 58 is considered normal. Timing can be influenced by variables such as ethnicity, weight, smoking, and number of pregnancies.

As hormone levels change many symptoms may occur; however, it is difficult to know which are due to changes in hormones and which are simply due to aging. Symptoms that may or may not be experienced are hot flashes, sleep problems, a change in sex drive, or mood changes. Some symptoms will last for months and others years. After a full year without a period, menopause is over, and the woman is infertile.

Not all women experience the same symptoms, and some experience more negative symptoms than others. Different cultures have different perceptions of menopause. Some view it as a time women acquire wisdom, whereas others view it as a time women "go crazy." Cultural values about aging are part of these beliefs. For example, in Asian cultures, elderly adults are given tremendous respect; consequently, most Asian women view menopause in a positive light. In contrast, Western cultures equate beauty with youth, and most women view menopause more negatively.

Some women seek "treatment" for menopause. Some of these treatments may temporarily alleviate symptoms, but the best "treatment" is exercise and a healthy diet. Long-term effects of hormone or medication therapies are largely unknown.

Is There a Male Menopause?
Males also experience age-related hormonal changes, but these changes are distinctly different from menopause. Beginning around age 30, production of testosterone declines slightly each year, but not until age 70 is the loss dramatic. The production of testosterone never stops completely; testes can continue to produce testosterone, and therefore are capable of sperm production well into the 80s.

Like women, however, men also experience changes in sleep, energy, sexual functioning, and mood. And just like with women, it is unclear which symptoms are due to hormonal changes and which are due to aging.

THE NERVOUS SYSTEM AND BRAIN DEVELOPMENT
During adulthood the brain changes, but for most healthy individuals the changes are minor and do not impact everyday functioning. Brain weight increases from birth until about age 30. After age 30 there is very gradual and slight weight loss in the brain; in later years brain weight loss accelerates. Some research suggests that different parts of the brain lose varying numbers of neurons. Some have hypothesized that patterns of neuronal loss are associated with comparable losses in abilities, causing problems such as memory loss and balance difficulties.

Other neurologists disagree, arguing that research on neuronal loss is flawed. They suggest there is growing evidence that neurons can regenerate and that many individuals between 60 and 90 show no noticeable neuronal loss. They posit that previous findings were based on studies with individuals who were sick and that the observed neuron loss was attributable to illness or disease rather than aging.

Regardless of the research, many older adults worry their brains are not as powerful as they once were. They report "senior moments" when they cannot recall information that should be known. It is tempting to blame cognitive difficulties on a flawed brain, but scientists studying the adult brain have

The Framingham Heart Study

In 1948 the Framingham Heart Study (FHS) began a longitudinal study of more than 5,000 adults from Framingham, Massachusetts. Researchers sought to better understand lifestyle habits related to heart disease. In 1971 children of the original participants were added to the study cohort; grandchildren entered the study in 2002. Having three generations of participants from one community in a single study is extremely rare and extremely fortuitous as it allows researchers to address many questions that cannot be answered by typical traditional studies.

Almost immediately, the study produced important findings. As early as the 1960s the FHS made significant contributions to a better understanding of heart disease. Links between heart disease and cigarettes, cholesterol, blood pressure, physical activity, and obesity were discovered. Later researchers studied other things, such as genetics, protective factors (like HDL cholesterol), and personality types.

Heart disease has not been the only condition studied. Researchers have also explored Alzheimer's, dementia, stroke, and other neurological conditions. They have also examined how conditions can spread throughout a social network—from one family member to another, and then from one friend to another.

The FHS has been one of the most influential longitudinal studies in medical history. It popularized the concept of risk factors and resulted in prediction equations that are still used today. Moreover, an understanding of risk factors has led to efforts to prevent heart disease, ultimately cutting death rates from heart attack and stroke in half. Today there are many longitudinal studies in progress, but the FHS was groundbreaking because it began when longitudinal studies were relatively rare and studied individuals from the same families and community, thus allowing researchers the unique opportunity to study both nature (biology and genetics) and nurture (the environment).

found the brain is more competent than once thought and that so-called "senior moments" are common to all ages.

Conflicting positions (one viewing the aging brain as increasingly feeble and the other arguing that brain competence remains stable) leaves students wondering, "Which position is correct?" As with many debates, a centrist position is probably best. Research has shown that the brain compensates for loss. For example, older adults use more regions of the brain, show more communication across the two hemispheres, and ultimately perform better at many cognitive tasks than younger adults do. And when compared to young adults, middle age adults are significantly better and faster at identifying main points of a complex problem, seeing patterns, and finding solutions.

There is also increasing evidence that neurons will sprout additional axons and dendrites during later years, thereby increasing or maintaining the overall number of synapses. This **compensatory sprouting**, combined with the fact that the brain develops with a great deal of redundancy, means the elderly brain exhibits more flexibility than once thought.

Fostering Brain Health
Several factors contribute to brain health, including low-calorie diets, an active social life, and tackling challenging cognitive tasks. Beyond these factors, the best way to support the aging brain is to maintain overall cardiovascular health. Arthur Kramer and his colleagues conducted a number of studies that recruited senior "couch potatoes" and randomly assigned them into two types of exercise groups that met three times a week: a cardiovascular group that walked, and a stretching and toning group. Measuring brain activity before and after the study found that the walkers had more brain activity, demonstrated better coordination of different parts of the brain, and did significantly better on cognitive tests. The brain volume of workers also changed. This research suggests physical activity is important, and that even unfit adults can change their brain volume and functionality.

COGNITIVE DEVELOPMENT
Understanding cognitive development during adulthood is complicated. First of all, there are many aspects of cognitive functioning, making it difficult to describe a single trend in development. Additionally, cognitive development is influenced by biological, psychological, social, and cultural factors, and this results in many different developmental paths. But the biggest limitation is that there is very little research on the topic. Most theorists fail to describe development past adolescence, and most research is done on students. When cognitive change is studied in adults, it is usually in relation to a decline in function.

Cohort Effects
Early developmentalists used intelligence tests to explore age-related changes in cognition. Many of these studies looked at groups of different-aged individuals. These studies found that intelligence peaks around 35, drops steadily until 65, and then shows rapid decline. In contrast, longitudinal studies that followed the same individuals over time found gains in intelligence. This difference is probably the result of **cohort effects.**

A cohort is a group of individuals who share something in common, usually year of birth. Cross-sectional studies compare individuals of different ages, but this generally means people born at different points in history. So an individual born in 1930 may be compared to an individual born in 1960. In 1930 the infant mortality rate was 6 percent, and 30 percent of teens graduated from high school. In 1960 infant mortality was 2.5 percent, and 70 percent of teens graduated from high school. If differences were found between these two groups, would they be due to age or to cohort?

As this example illustrates, it is impossible to draw conclusions about age differences when comparing individuals from different cohorts, because they are also different with respect to a number of other variables, including nutrition, health, and education. Longitudinal studies can also be criticized because they look at individuals from only one cohort. A longitudinal study of individuals born in 1960 yields information only about individuals born in 1960. These problems can be remedied with cross-sequential research.

Werner Schaie conducted a cross-sequential study of intelligence that began in 1956, using a cross-section of individuals aged 25, 32, 39, 46, 53, 60, and 67 years. Each participant took an intelligence test. Every 7 years, for the next 35 years, a subset of the sample was retested; more samples were added in later years. From these data Schaie made cross-sectional and longitudinal comparisons. Cross-sectional comparisons showed a steady drop in IQ beginning at age 25. Longitudinal comparisons showed IQ increases during early adulthood remained constant until age 60 and then declined. This trend was found for all age cohorts, indicating that year of birth did not influence the longitudinal results.

Intelligence: Fluid and Crystallized

One way to explain the issue of developmental change is to define intelligence as more than one general factor. Psychologists John Horn and Raymond Cattell proposed two types of intelligence, fluid and crystallized. **Fluid intelligence** refers to the ability to think and solve new problems. It is the foundation of logical problem solving and relies on skills such as processing speed and the ability to see patterns and relationships among variables. One way to test fluid intelligence is to present a series of letters (for example, D, H, L) and ask which letter comes next (the answer is P).

Crystallized intelligence depends on accumulated knowledge and experience, including education. Vocabulary use and comprehension, general information, and logical reasoning are all types of crystallized intelligence. Although fluid and crystallized intelligence are separate abilities, they tend to be related. Most individuals with high fluid intelligence also have high crystallized intelligence.

Studies have found crystallized intelligence increases throughout middle adulthood. Beginning in the 20s fluid intelligence begins to decline, and tasks such as recalling letters become increasingly more difficult. Some scientists believe the decline mirrors changes in the brain and nervous system.

Wisdom

Elderly people continue to learn new things. Their problem solving is more thoughtful and less distracted by emotions and impulses. Moreover, they have been around longer and have thus accumulated more knowledge. **Wisdom** involves having knowledge and the ability to apply it to everyday problems. It is using good judgment. Wisdom is not a direct product of old age, but having done many things increases the chances of wisdom. It is a concept described by just about every culture and historical period, and yet there is little research on the topic.

Memory and Memory Loss

Memory is another important aspect of thinking. From age 20 through 60, the amount of information that can be retained in short-term memory decreases. This can be measured by giving someone a list of words or numbers to recall, or by asking someone to read and recall text. Amount of loss is related to how memory is measured, so for example there is less loss in the ability to remember prose than in the ability to remember lists of things. When time pressure is removed there are no age differences. So short-term memory loss is evident only with certain tasks and under certain conditions.

Memory Loss

Medical or mental health conditions, such as depression or the side-effects of medication, can cause memory loss. Sometimes memory loss is due to a change in the brain. **Dementia** is a group of neurological disorders involving memory and cognitive loss. An estimated 13 percent of adults over the age of 65 suffer with dementia, and rates increase with age. The condition is reversible for some, but for most it is not. Nor can it be cured. Dementia is caused by damage to the brain. Many things can causes such damage, including head injury, alcohol, or diseases such as Parkinson's. The two most common causes of dementia are Alzheimer's disease and strokes.

Alzheimer's disease is a specific type of dementia. The cause remains unknown; however, genetics often plays a role. Age of onset varies, as does the rate at which symptoms emerge. There is no cure, and treatment involves slowing progression of symptoms. Early symptoms are usually severe memory problems, such as forgetting names or how to do familiar activities. Depression usually follows. Delusions and sleep disturbances also emerge, as do extremes in emotions such as anger, or dependency and clinginess. Memory impairment becomes progressively worse, with memories of recent events lost before memories of long-ago events. Physical movements become increasingly more difficult. The course of the disease can vary. Some individuals with Alzheimer's may live a short time, whereas others live much longer.

Although the cause of Alzheimer's remains unknown, what is known is that brain damage occurred. Researchers are searching for ways to prevent Alzheimer's. Some evidence suggests a "Mediterranean diet" high in vegetables, fish, and olive oil is helpful. Education may be a protective factor because there are lower rates of Alzheimer's among people with more education. Having an active social life and regular and varied physical activities are also associated with decreased risk.

SOCIAL AND EMOTIONAL DEVELOPMENT
Social and emotional development during adulthood is both complicated and poorly understood. Most theoretical and empirical work in the field has been done either at the beginning of adulthood (prior to age 25) or toward the end (after age 60) of life. Developmentalists know the least about the largest segment of the lifespan. What is known is that adulthood is more complicated than once thought.

Erikson's Psychosocial Stages
Erik Erikson (1902–1994) extended the work of Sigmund Freud, but unlike Freud's psychosexual stages, Erikson's psychosocial stages cover the entire lifespan and recognize the impact of history, society, and culture on personality. Each of Erikson's eight stages has a "crisis" to be resolved. The crises are turning points that if mastered will lead to higher levels of development; if not mastered, they will reemerge during later life stages. But Erikson's theory is optimistic, positing that it is possible to master a crisis from an earlier stage.

The stage Erikson is most famous for is *Identity versus Role Confusion* (see Chapter 6). This stage is associated with adolescence, a time when individuals must develop a sense of self in order to develop their own personal identities or fall prey to role confusion.

During early adulthood, the crisis is *Intimacy versus Isolation.* Young adults must form an intimate, loving relationship with a partner. Not doing so leads to loneliness and isolation. Erikson believed young adults must have their own sense of self before successfully merging their identity with another person. He also noted women often form an identity after finding a partner. In other words, Erikson's theory was more applicable to male development than female development. But most women today adopt a career prior to marriage, and the average age of marriage has increased. So contemporary psychologists suggest the path to identity and intimacy is more similar for women and men than it was in the past.

During middle adulthood the crisis is *Generativity versus Stagnation.* Whether through work or family, adults need to create or nurture things that will outlast them. Success results in feelings of accomplishment, but failure leads to a sense of loss. A number of studies have found adults in their 40s are interested in raising or mentoring younger generations and seek to pass on something valuable. This, however, does not usually involve a "crisis."

The term **midlife crisis** was first used by Elliott Jaques in the 1960s and was popularized by Gail Sheehy in her book *Passages*. A midlife crisis is a time when an individual faces aging and mortality and ultimately wants to make life changes, such as leaving a job, ending a marriage, altering physical appearance, or reevaluating life goals. The research in this area is contradictory. Different studies have found that as few as 8 percent and as many as 80 percent of American men experience an age-related crisis. These differences are probably due to how "crisis" is defined by the research in question: Is it a period of trauma or a time of questioning? Unfortunately, most existing research on this topic is with men living in the United States, and it is impossible to draw conclusions about other groups.

Erikson's final stage centers on the *Integrity versus Despair* crisis. Older adults reflect on their life and search for meaning. Success leaves them with a sense of acquired wisdom and fulfillment, but failure leaves them with regret, bitterness, and despair.

On the whole, there has been support for Erikson's ideas about adult development. For example, research suggests identity in early adulthood predicts success in the later stages of intimacy, generativity, and integrity. But his ideas have also been criticized. Although Erikson is applauded for covering the entire lifespan, critics say his emphasis is clearly on childhood and that the theory is

Revisiting Tomas, Gregoria, and Armanda

Tomas and Gregoria have had continued success with their new home and farm. They were eventually able to purchase a yoke team and hire a young man to help Tomas with daily chores. Armanda has slowed down, but she continues to work with Gregoria in the kitchen.

After graduation, Aureila left Colomi and joined her brother in the capital city where she works as a bookkeeper. Gregoria and Tomas both feel a strong sense of pride and loss. Gregoria reflects, "This is what we worked for. This is everything we wanted. But, maybe we wanted too much."

Tomas agrees. "My children are a success, and that is the way it should be. But I am sad they are far away. It is not practical for us to visit, and we cannot expect them to visit us."

Armanda is much more prosaic. "If God wants those children in La Paz, then that is where they will be. They were too busy for us. Of course they will return, but first they need to start on their own path. That is what children do."

not as well developed for adults. Others contend that the theory best applies to Western males and does not generalize well across genders or cultures.

SOCIAL DEVELOPMENT

Adults adopt many roles: friend, spouse, parent, grandparent, and worker. But with the lifespan stretching longer and longer, new roles are emerging.

Friendships

The social world for adults mostly revolves around family and friends. Studies of friendships during adulthood are rare, and few longitudinal studies exist to clarify developmental changes in friendships. To further complicate the matter, existing data hints that friendships vary depending on sex, age, marital status, parental status, and employment.

Friendships are voluntary relationships between individuals of equal status, with the goal of mutual enjoyment and satisfaction. At different life stages, time spent with friends changes. Middle-age adults spend the least amount of time with friends, and newlyweds and older adults the most. But at every age, adults report the same function of friends: mutual enjoyment and trust. Studies of older adults have found life satisfaction and happiness are more closely linked to friends than to adult children.

Marriage

Finding a partner and maintaining a long-term intimate relationship is often considered one of the most fundamental aspects of adult development, particularly during early adulthood. Americans have one of the highest marriage rates in the world, and even after divorce, usually seek remarriage. A number of studies have found that married adults are happier, healthier, live longer, and have lower rates of mental health problems. Of course it is difficult to know if marriage causes these benefits, or if the positive variables are what makes it possible to sustain a marriage. More precise research has found marriage is not necessarily beneficial—the quality of marriage is what matters. Happy marriages make people happy and healthy; unhappy marriages do not.

In some cultures marriages are arranged by parents and are driven by economic or social forces. In Western cultures adults self-select mates through the process of dating. Western studies of mate selection reveal the variables related to initial attraction are not the same as those leading to commitment and surviving a long-term relationship.

Marital success is in part predicted by variables outside the marriage. Some examples of this are marrying at an older age, having parents who stayed married, attending religious services, and an intolerant attitude toward divorce. Marriages are more likely to fail when one or both partners are anxious, touchy, self-pitying, or easily hurt, angry, or jealous. However, just as important is the quality of interactions between partners. Researcher John Gottman found marriages last when good times outweigh bad. The number of negative interactions, such as complaints, criticism, or putdowns, is significantly less than the number of positive interactions. Fighting in and of itself does not predict divorce. Some couples in successful marriages bicker and disagree a lot, but balance this with laughter and affection.

Same-Sex Partners
Most research on marriage has involved heterosexual couples, but increasingly same-sex couples in long-term relationships are being studied. Evidence suggests that the characteristics predictive of stable heterosexual relationships also predict stability in homosexual couples—good times should outweigh the bad. And just like heterosexual adults, homosexual adults in long-term relationships show better physical and mental health and report a partner as being an important source of companionship and support.

Of course, lesbian and gay couples are not the same as heterosexual couples. To begin with, most same-sex couples cannot legally marry, nor can they "accidentally" become parents. Moreover, same-sex couples are highly likely to experience discrimination. There are also important demographic differences between homosexual and heterosexual couples. On average same-sex couples have shorter relationships, fewer children, and a more egalitarian division of labor. So making comparisons between these groups is a little like comparing apples to oranges. Nonetheless, existing evidence suggests that relationship stability variables are mostly the same regardless of sexual orientation.

Divorce
An often cited statistic is that 50 percent of U.S. marriages end in divorce; this compares the number of marriages and divorces in one year, so remarriages and second divorces are included. Studies following couples longitudinally reveal that about 20 percent of adults divorce, but those with one divorce are significantly more likely to have several. About two-thirds of divorced adults remarry, and remarriages are especially vulnerable to divorce.

Divorce is a major life stressor and is linked both to physical and emotional illnesses. There is also usually a significant economic impact. But most health effects are short-term. Less is known about long-term consequences. Research shows that 10 years after divorce, some people grew from the experience whereas others continued to suffer. Little is known about what predicts these varied responses.

Although the impact of divorce on divorced adults is poorly understood, there is a good deal known about the consequences of divorce for children. About 40 percent of children in the United States experience the divorce of parents. Mavis Hetherington has studied families longitudinally for up to 30 years and has found that most children whose parents divorced adjust well; but about one-fourth suffer into adulthood. They have less education and a lower socio-economic status than individuals whose parents stayed married. They also tend to have more mental health problems, and higher rates of divorce. For obvious reasons, this leaves parents who contemplate divorce wondering, "Should we stay married for the sake of the kids?" It may be a moot point. According to Hetherington, divorce is a process that begins long before separation and the consequences of this ongoing process linger years after the divorce itself. So the answer depends on how parents act around their children before, during, and after a divorce. Parents damage children by fighting in front of them, involving them in disagreements, asking them to take sides, or pitting them against the other parent. So whether parents stay married and fight or get divorced and fight, it is still damaging. The act of divorce is not as important as how parents behave. When parents treat each other with civility and respect, regardless of their marital status, children do well.

Widowhood

Widowhood refers to the death of a life-partner. Research indicates that the impact is greatest in the year following the loss. Immune system function-ing is low and depression and anxiety are high. Of course, relationships vary.

Revisiting Suzette and David

Divorce is everywhere. Of course this is wrong, but it's reality. I'm David. My mom and dad divorced my freshman year in high school. My sister Suzette was too young to understand, but it was because my mom had an affair. Nobody ever talks about it.

I couldn't tell you how many places we moved to during high school. At first I lived with my mom. But nothing was ever stable, and I wanted to go to the same high school. I was flunking everything and got in trouble with the cops. I had to work so we had money for food. Then I went with my dad, and everything got better.

My mother stopped speaking to me when I moved in with my dad. But then she remarried and things calmed down. When Suzette got pregnant they were all mad at her. My step-father kicked her out, and my dad stopped talking to her, and my mom went along with everyone else. What hypocrites.

I'm almost 21 and I don't talk about anything because I feel like anyone I talk to won't understand my life. My sister is the most normal person in the fam-ily. I am glad my grandparents are there for us. Without them we would have nobody. They are not self-centered like my parents.

Differences in age when the loss occurred, suddenness of loss, quality of relationship, coping style of survivor, and pragmatic variables, such as economic circumstances, can vary. There can be tremendous differences in how severe the effects are and how long they last.

From a developmental perspective, one important factor to consider is age. Young spouses experience loss differently than older spouses do. The death of a young partner disrupts the anticipated life course. There is usually little time to prepare, and survivors are left with heavy financial and parenting responsibilities. Additionally, there are few role models to show survivors how to adjust. Most eventually adjust well.

Singlehood

Singlehood means living without an intimate partner. Its frequency has increased, although actual rates are unknown because no federal agency tracks singlehood. It is estimated 8 to 10 percent of adults stay single. Some choose singlehood, perhaps focusing on a career; others are single due to circumstances, such as not finding "the right person."

As with other social roles, single adults with more social support are happier than those with less. Most report they are content and have active social lives. Many have periods of stress, such as when peers marry and have children; for women, the approach of menopause is a known stressor. Childless adults often manage to play important roles in the lives of younger people, such as nieces, nephews, or children of friends. Moreover, an increasing number of women now become parents without partners, either through a temporary relationship, medically assisted fertilization, or adoption. This phenomenon is fairly new, and there is little research on this group of women.

Work

"What do you do?" is one of the first questions people ask when meeting someone new. Employment is a key aspect of one's sense of self, and most adults spend a large amount of time working. Numerous studies show job satisfaction is lowest in early adulthood and rises steadily until retirement. In part, this is a function of the amount of time spent in a particular job. Having a job longer usually means more pay, more responsibility, and more security. Younger employees are usually assigned jobs that are more physically demanding and less interesting.

Juggling Work and Family

Most parents with children, as well as adult children caring for aging parents, are also in the workforce. Although both women and men experience stress over juggling the responsibilities of family and work, this stress is more pronounced for women. **Role overload** occurs when individuals have difficulty

When Do Adults Stop Having Sex?

There are many myths and stereotypes about sexuality, many of them created and promoted by the media. Television programs and movies, for example, are more likely to show unmarried adults having sex than married adults; in real life, married people have more sex than unmarried people. Sex in the media is also depicted as occurring spontaneously, leaving no time to plan for birth control; in reality most couples know intercourse is about to happen and plan accordingly. Media myths and stereotypes related to sexuality during later adulthood abound. The media, for example, frequently depicts young adults as sexual beings and older adults as decrepit beings that need a pill to "enhance performance."

Despite media stereotypes, sexual ability for both males and females continues well into the 80s. There is not much research about the 90s, and some of the research is limited because elderly adults often live alone or lack partners. On average males die younger than females; hence it becomes difficult for unmarried senior females to find partners.

For those with partners, longitudinal research shows that frequency of sexual activity declines slightly with age but remains more or less stable with respect to pattern of frequency. In other words, couples that have frequent sex during early adulthood, are likely to have frequent sex in middle and later adulthood. The majority of long-term couples over age 50 report more spontaneity, fewer inhibitions, and more freedom in their sex lives. They also report that sex is an important component of their relationship. The research on sex and aging shows two main findings. The first is that regular sexual activity is important for maintaining sexual functioning (the use-it-or-lose-it principle). Sexual organs that are more often stimulated respond more easily than those which are rarely stimulated (regardless of who is doing the stimulation, self or other). The second finding is that general health is important to sexuality. Those in better health, especially cardiovascular health, tend to engage in more sexual activity.

Whereas many aspects of physical activity tend to decline during later adulthood, the physiological ability to respond sexually does not diminish with age and sexuality remains an important aspect of adult development. Older men and older women simply need more time to become aroused and achieve orgasm.

managing the numerous roles they occupy. Research shows benefits to having both work and family responsibilities; these include a better standard of living, happier marriages, and greater life satisfaction. Overload most often occurs when employees lack control over conflicting responsibilities. When jobs are more family friendly—allowing employees to choose start and stop times, having flexible leave policies, or providing child or elder care assistance—workers are less stressed and more productive.

Unemployment

Unemployment mostly affects those at the start of their careers or people who have reached middle-age or are older. Many companies have a "last hired, first fired" policy, which often leaves young workers bouncing from one job to another. But when companies downsize, it is the higher paying jobs that are lost, leaving middle-aged workers especially vulnerable. Conversely, this age group is least likely to be hired, so finding employment after a job loss is challenging.

Older and younger workers decline in physical and mental health after the loss of a job, but this decline is significantly greater and can last much longer for middle-aged workers. Social support is important.

Retirement

With a longer life expectancy (about 76 for men and 81 for women), time spent in retirement has lengthened. Today the most common age to retire in the United States is 62, but many people continue to work past this age for financial reasons or because they love their jobs. On the other hand, some workers are forced into retirement for health reasons or because of downsizing; this may happen at or before age 62. An increasing subgroup of retirees is **quasi-retired**. These adults ease their way into retirement by reducing work hours or by becoming independent consultants or contractors.

In industrialized nations most governments offer pensions that ensure a sufficient standard of living. In the United States, however, federally funded social security usually means a retiree's income drops about 50 percent unless other financial preparations were made. Most seniors do not fall into poverty during retirement, but there are significant differences in post-retirement standards of living across gender and ethnic groups.

Another sometimes unpleasant aspect of retirement is loss of job status. This occurs because identity and self-esteem are so closely linked with work. Some retirees find it difficult to find things to do with their newly acquired free time; some miss the work and/or the mental and physical stimulation it provided. Although loss of work can be traumatic, research shows that for most retirees (about 66 to 90 percent) life satisfaction, mental health, and physical health do not decline. In fact, retirement is viewed as a time to follow old interests or find new ones. The best predictor of happiness during retirement is having a plan to stay busy, whether engaging in leisure pursuits, volunteer work, or other activities.

Living Arrangements of Older Adults

An increasing trend among older adults is life in residential communities for seniors; approximately 15 percent of U.S. seniors have chosen this option. Some of these communities include **assisted-living** arrangements, which provide residents with support services, including meals, group activities, and supervision as needed. Research shows that such communities generally have positive effects on physical and mental health. A key benefit is social support from staff and residents. One detriment is expense.

How Important Is Personal Control?

In the 1970s psychologists knew the mind and body were connected but were not sure how or how much. To study this, Ellen Langer and Judith Rodin looked at personal control in nursing home residents. They went to a nursing home with four floors where all residents were in frail health. They randomly selected two floors for the treatment group and two other floors to serve as the comparison group. Residents were to complete a pre-test questionnaire about how much control they felt and how active and happy they were. Nurses also rated each patient's happiness, alertness, independence, sociability, and activity.

After the pre-test was administered, the nursing home director met with both groups. He told residents in the treatment group they were responsible for their own care and how they spent their time. They could arrange their rooms, select when to see a movie, and were offered a plant to care for.

The director told the comparison group the nursing home was responsible for making their lives full, interesting, and happy, so decisions would be made by the nurses. Nurses scheduled the movies, arranged rooms, and cared for plants given to residents.

After three weeks, residents and nurses completed the questionnaires again. Then all residents in the facility were given the same policies as the treatment group (i.e., all residents were told they were responsible for their own care and how they spent their time). There was one difference in the delivery of this information; in the case of the treatment group, the policies were repeated and made clearer.

Results indicated the treatment group felt happier and were more active than the comparison group. Between pre- and post-tests, nurses thought the treatment group improved, but the comparison group declined. Eighteen months later, nurses and doctors again rated the residents. The treatment group had better health ratings. But, the most surprising finding was that 30 percent of participants in the comparison group had died, while only 15 percent from the treatment group died, a clear indication that control over one's own life is linked to health.

Since Langer and Rodin's study, numerous others have found similar results. Adults stay healthier when they have a sense of control over their lives, especially when placed in situations where there is a loss of control.

When seniors have high needs for care, nursing homes are also an option. About 5 percent of U.S. seniors receive nursing home care. For some, this is a long-term arrangement, but many leave once high care needs become unnecessary. Nursing homes, like adult residential communities and assisted-living facilities, can be costly. In the United States, these are out-of-pocket costs, and the expense can quickly deplete the savings of elderly adults, leaving them financially dependent on their family, or reliant on the minimal financial support provided by social security. Sadly, the quality of care is often linked to the cost, leaving the poorest adults to suffer in low-quality institutions.

Death and Dying
The topic of death and dying is not often discussed in Western cultures even though these are natural processes and inevitable for all who were born. Medical advances have postponed death for many, leaving ethical and philosophical questions about the quality of life and the dignity of death.

In industrialized nations, death for young people is usually the result of unintentional injury and is usually unexpected (one exception is in times of war). For about a quarter of adults, death also occurs suddenly or shortly after symptoms appear (for example, when someone has a heart attack). But for about 75 percent of adults, there is time to prepare, especially when they know death is coming from illness or disease.

What is Death?
Death used to be defined as occurring when breathing and heartbeat stopped. Today, medical technology can keep the heart and lungs working. **Brain death** occurs when the brain shows no activity. But if a machine keeps the heart and lungs working, is that life? It becomes even more complicated when only part of the brain works. **Persistent vegetative state** is when the brain stem (which is responsible for vital functions) works but the cortex does not. The individual in this state requires a feeding tube but may exhibit evidence of basic reflexes, such as a sleep-wake cycle. But without a working cortex there is no awareness. Some doctors consider this death, but others point to rare instances when cortical brain activity has returned, sometimes after months of no activity. The debate is mainly over how long the brain can be in a vegetative state before it can no longer regain functioning.

There are many different ways to respond to one's impending death. In the 1960s Elizabeth Kübler-Ross proposed a series of stages, including denial, anger, and depression, that occur en route to accepting death. Contemporary psychologists recognize the contributions of Kübler-Ross, but today these stages are usually thought of as coping strategies and not stages because there are many different ways to face death.

CONCLUSION

Compared to other life stages, adulthood lasts a long time. Although there is much decline in physical development, lifestyle choice can mediate this decline. Additionally, the aging brain shows remarkable competence. Whereas it was once thought that age resulted in deficits in cognitive development, it is now known that cognitive abilities continue to mature and that even the very old can learn new things. Adults engage in numerous identities, and each new role has the potential to contribute positively to life satisfaction.

A phrase repeated several times in this chapter is *more research is needed.* Adulthood remains a fairly new field of study, and often only clinical conditions are studied, which means that atypical development is better understood than typical development. A second oft-repeated phrase from this chapter is *it depends.* During adulthood, contexts can vary tremendously, and variables like gender, age, marital status, parental status, employment status, sexual orientation, socioeconomic status, and cultural background can all impact development tremendously. Humans are **resilient**—capable of coping effectively despite overwhelming risk factors. In psychology, there are few causes and effects. Usually there are complex interactions. So although there may be risk factors in all aspects of life, it is important to remember that the right combination of protective factors at the right time can outweigh most potential risks.

Further Reading

Atabiner, Karen. "Strengthening Older Muscles." *The New York Times* (January 18, 2011). Accessed August 1, 2011; available from http://newoldage.blogs.nytimes.com/2011/01/18/strengthening-older-muscles/?ref=elderly

Dallas, Mary Elizabeth. "Study Finds Self-esteem Levels Vary by Age, Race." *USA Today* (July 22, 2011). Accessed August 1, 2011; available from http://yourlife.usatoday.com/mind-soul/story/2011/07Study-finds-self-esteem-levels-vary-by-age-race/49606266/1

Doctors Without Borders. Available at http://www.doctorswithoutborders.org/

Framingham Heart Study. Available at http://www.framinhamheartstudy.org.

Gibbs, Nancy. "Midlife Crisis? Bring It On!" *Time* (May 8, 2005) accessed August 1, 2011; available from http://www.time.com/time/magazine/article/0,9171,1059032,00.html#ixzz1UYJUitc0

Gottman, J. *Why Marriages Succeed or Fail… and How you can make yours last.* New York, NY: Simon & Schuster, 1994.

Hetherington, E.M. and Kelly, J. *For Better or For Worse: Divorce Reconsidered.* New York NY: W.W. Norton & Company, 2003.

National Institute on Aging. Available at http://www.nia.nih.gov/

O'Connor, Anahad. "Centenarians Have Plenty of Bad Habits Too." *The New York Times* (August 4, 2011), accessed 5 August 2011; available from http://well.blogs.nytimes .com/2011/08/04/centenarians-have-plenty-of-bad-habits-too/?ref=elderly

Sheehy, G. Passages: Predictable crises of adult life. Bantam Books, 1976.

Society for Research in Adult Development. Available at http://www.adultdevelopment .org/

GLOSSARY

achievement gap   A difference between groups of students who should not differ, such as rich and poor, black and white, disabled and non-disabled.

adolescence   The life stage occurring after childhood and before adulthood, usually beginning at puberty and ending when an individual is fully responsible for self.

adulthood   The life stage that begins after adolescence and lasts until death.

age of viability   The earliest time a fetus is likely to survive being born. Usually about 23 weeks and mostly contingent on medical assistance.

Alzheimer's disease   A specific type of dementia.

amniocentesis   A prenatal genetic test that uses ultrasound to guide the insertion of a needle through the mother's abdomen and into the uterus to remove a sample of amniotic fluid.

Apgar score   A screening assessment; conducted 1 and 5 minutes after birth, it gives a general idea of the newborn's health.

Asperger's Syndrome   A type of developmental disorder characterized by poor social understanding and extreme attention to details.

assisted living   A group living situation where residents have support services, which include meals, supervision, and common activities.

assisted reproductive technology (ART)   A general term describing medical procedures used to help a couple get pregnant

associative play   A type of play that occurs when children play similarly, share materials, and talk to each, but do not coordinate games or activities.

asynchrony   Growth or body development that is not concurrent; when parts of the of the body do not develop at the same rate or at the same time.

attachment   An enduring emotional bond to another person.

attention deficit hyperactivity disorder (ADHD)   A condition that causes difficulty concentrating or paying attention, as well as impulsive and overly active behavior.

authoritarian   A parenting style characterized by high control and maturity demands, and low communication and warmth.

authoritative   A parenting style characterized by clear (but sometimes flexible) rules and consequences if rules are broken, high communication.

autism   A developmental disorder characterized by problems with language and unusual ways of relating to people or objects.

autonomy versus shame and doubt   Erikson's second psychosocial crisis during which toddlers learn self-confidence and independence or become dependent and lack confidence.

axons   A part of the neuron that carries electrical signals and sends messages to other neurons.

babbling   Consonant vowel combinations made by babies that are repeated over and over (e.g., ba-ba-ba).

baby boomers   Individuals born between 1946 and 1964.

Back-to-Sleep campaign   An educational campaign designed to lower rates of SIDS by encouraging parents to put infants to sleep on their backs, not their stomachs.

basal metabolism   Rate at which calories burn when the body is at rest.

behaviorism   A class of theories that study directly observable events and behaviors. Sometimes called learning theories because they describe ways behaviors are learned.

biological aging   Biologically determined declines in body functioning.

birth   The passing of a fetus from the uterus.

birth order   The age position siblings hold in a family, usually ranked, oldest, middle, or youngest but difficult to determine in certain family structures (blended families, families with large aged differences, etc.)

bi-sexual   Sexually attracted to both males and females.

brain death   A condition marked by the absence of any brain activity while a machine keeps the heart and lungs working.

Bucharest Early Intervention Project   A longitudinal research project that recruited and trained foster parents to raise children who had previously experienced severe deprivation.

center of gravity The place on the body where weight is equally divided above and below that point.

centration Children focusing on the most obvious aspect of a problem, or only one aspect of a problem.

cephalocaudal principle Growth occurs from the head downward.

cerebellum A part of the lower brain involved in movement and related functions.

Cesarean section A surgical method of childbirth; an incision is made through the mother's abdomen and uterus to remove the baby.

child-directed speech Adult speech directed at children; characterized by short utterances, a high-pitch, clear pronunciation, exaggerated expressions and gestures, and repetition.

chorionic villi sampling (CVS) A genetic test utilizing a needle to remove a small piece of villi that attaches the amniotic sac to the uterine wall.

chromosomal abnormalities Illnesses or conditions caused by damaged chromosomes or mutations in chromosomes.

class inclusion The understanding that one group can be part of a larger group.

classical conditioning The learning process that results from the association between something meaningful and something neutral.

cliques Small groups of friends who are loyal to each other and do many things together.

cognitive theories A class of theories that emphasize developmental changes in mental processes, such as logic, memory, and language.

cohort A group of individuals who share some historical experience, such as year of birth.

cohort effect A problem that occurs in a study when cohorts of individuals who should be the same on some variable are not.

coming-out Also referred to as coming-out-of-the-closet; steps taken to tell others about one's sexual orientation or gender identity.

commitment The extent to which one shows a personal investment in roles and beliefs.

compensatory sprouting When neurons grow additional axons and dendrites during adulthood, thus increasing or maintaining the overall number of synapses.

comprehensive An approach to intervention and prevention; this approach involves many modes of communication and is directed at attempts to change many aspects of risk behavior.

concrete operations   The Piagetian stage of cognitive development that lasts from about 7 to 11; the time when mental abilities become more logical with respect to things that are real, solid, and visible.

conservation   Understanding that the properties of an object stay the same, even if there is a change in appearance.

context   The personal or environmental circumstances that influence an individual, including family, media, and historical time period.

coo   Drawn out vowel sound made by babies; usually occur when a baby is happy.

cooperative play   A type of play that occurs among a group of children who have a common goal with a clear division of roles among group members.

corpus callosum   A bundle of nerve fibers that connect the left and right sides (hemispheres) of the cortex, enabling communication between the hemispheres.

cortex   The gray matter on the outside part of the brain, which is responsible for perception, body movement, thinking, language, and memory.

co-sleeping   Parents and baby sleeping in the same bed or in close proximity.

criterion-referenced test   A test whose scores are compared to a specific criteria, or a previously determined standard set by a group of experts.

critical period   A time period when something is especially susceptible to influence but only if exposed to some trigger in the environment at this time.

cross-sectional research   A research method that examines different age groups at one time.

crowds   Large reputation-based groups of individuals who are not necessarily friends and do not necessarily spend time together, but share some characteristic that identifies them as part of the group.

crystallized intelligence   Thinking that uses accumulated knowledge and experience.

cycle of abuse   A pattern of abuse that emerges when abused children grow up to be abusive adults.

dementia   A group of neurological disorders that involve memory and cognitive loss.

dendrites   Bushy fibers that shoot off a cell body and pick up messages from other neurons.

development   Changes in the physical size, cognitive abilities, and social and emotional status of an individual.

developmental disability   An umbrella classification for conditions that begin during childhood and are characterized by mental or physical impairments.

developmental psychology   The scientific study of the human mind, behavior, and emotions, and how they change over time.

developmentalists   Social scientists, educators, medical professionals, and clinicians who study human development.

differentiation   A characteristic of cells that occurs during prenatal development when cells become specialized and take on specific roles

diffused   A term describing an individual who has neither explored nor committed to a sense of identity.

dishabituation   A phenomenon that occurs after habituating to something (i.e., becoming desensitized to a repeated stimulus); if a new stimuli is presented and there is an increase in response, it indicates the difference was noticed.

Down's syndrome   Also called trisomy-21, a condition that occurs when instead of having two twenty-first chromosomes, the individual has three. The syndrome is characterized by a number of distinct physical manifestations, including a round face and flat nose, as well as medical problems and cognitive disabilities.

early childhood   The time period between age 2 and age 5, sometimes called the preschool or play years.

eclectic perspective   An approach that uses multiple theories to explain development.

ecological perspective   The view that individuals should be studied within all the contexts and interactions in which they live.

egocentrism   A Piagetian term for the tendency of children to view the world from their own perspective.

embryo   The human organism during the embryonic period.

embryonic period   The period of pregnancy that begins at implantation and lasts through the eighth week of pregnancy.

emotional abuse   Ongoing belittling, insulting, berating, or ignoring another individual.

empiricism   Something based on observable experiences, experimentation, or data.

epidural   Medication injected into the spine to eliminate feeling from that point in the spine downward while allowing the patient to remain alert; often used to make childbirth less painful for mothers.

ethological theories   A class of theories that propose behaviors evolve in a species to ensure the survival of the species.

evolutionary theory   Theory that species or individuals who best meet the demands of the environment survive long enough to reproduce, and those less suited to the environment die off.

expectancy effects   The influence of a researcher's expectations on the outcome of a study; *see also* self fulfilling prophecy.

exploration   A time during which one questions "self," basic moral beliefs, interpersonal styles, habits, and life goals.

expressive language   The production of meaningful language.

family functioning   How well a family meets the needs of its members.

family structure   The legal, biological, and practical relationships between and among family members.

fast-mapping   A quick way to link words together in mental categories, based on how the words are used.

feedback loop   When the output of one system triggers the start or inhibition of another.

fertilization   When the ovum (egg) and sperm unite, sometimes called conception.

fetal alcohol syndrome (FAS)   A cluster of lifelong mental and physical symptoms including distinct facial features, slowed growth, small head, and slowed intellectual and behavioral development that result from the mother drinking alcohol during pregnancy.

fetal period   A period that begins at the ninth week of pregnancy and lasts until delivery.

fetus   The developing human organism during the fetal period.

fine motor skills   Small body movements.

fluid intelligence   The ability to think and solve new problems.

foreclosed   An individual who has made commitments to an identity but has done so without a period of exploration and questioning

formal operations   Piaget's final stage of cognitive development, which begins around age 12 and is characterized by any abstract hypothetical thought.

friend's influence   A subtle form of peer pressure where friends encourage each other to conform to the group in either positive or negative ways.

friendship   A relationship mutually valued by both partners.

frontal lobe   A region of the brain situated behind the forehead and responsible for functions such as problem solving, decision making, movement, emotions, and impulse control.

gay   Homosexual males; sometimes refers to all homosexual individuals.

gender identity   Personal sense of self as male or female, including acceptance of gender roles and stereotypes.

generalize   Applying the results of a study to people who were not in the study.

generativity versus stagnation   Erikson's seventh stage, which occurs during middle adulthood and involves the need to create or nurture things that will outlast the individual.

genetic counseling   Consultation and medical testing that occurs when a couple wants information about their genetic heritage and conditions that might be passed on to children.

genetic diseases   Illnesses carried by biological parents and passed down from one generation to the next.

germinal period   The first two weeks of pregnancy, beginning with fertilization and ending with implantation; a time of rapid cell division

gestural language   Gestures and non-word sounds as communicative devices.

glial cells   Cells that support the brain and are sometimes called the glue of the brain; glial cells insulate, provide oxygen and nutrients, and provide structure to the brain.

globalization   An increasingly common socialization that results from the rapid sharing of information around the world.

gonads   The organ that produces the sex cells, testes in males and ovaries in females.

gross motor skills   Large body movements.

growth   An increase in body size and weight.

growth curve table   A graph that shows averages of growth (norms) at different ages.

growth spurts   Periods of rapid growth in a brief span of time.

guided participation   A technique from sociocultural theory in which mentors present younger learners with work that is challenging yet attainable, help and provide instruction if needed, and encourage and motivate the learner.

habituation   When a stimuli is presented over and over the initial reaction lessens.

Harlem Children's Zone   An intervention project in an area of Harlem, New York, which provides a variety of educational, social, medical, and community services for children and their families and is designed to improve the well-being of the community.

Head Start   A federally funded program that provides poor children with preschool and adequate nutrition, dental, and health services; the program requires parents to participate by contributing to program planning, working in the classroom, or attending adult programs.

heterosexual   Sexually attracted to the opposite sex.

homosexual   Sexually attracted to others of the same sex.

hypothalamus   A part of the brain that controls things like hunger, thirst, and sleep-wake cycles; it also produces certain hormones.

hypothetical-deductive reasoning   The process of considering what might affect the outcome of a problem and then systematically testing possibilities.

identity achieved   An individual who has made commitments to social roles, personal beliefs, values, and life goals after going through a period of questioning and exploration.

identity crisis   A time of struggle during which the individual makes role choices and decides upon a belief and value system.

identity versus role confusion   Erikson's fifth psychosocial stage which describes adolescence as the time to answer the questions Who am I? Were am I going? Who am I to become?

imaginary audience   A term that describes adolescents' belief that others pay a great deal of attention to them, making them feel as if they are on a stage and constantly watched.

immunization   A small dose of inactive virus administered to stimulate the immune system, thus allowing the body to fight off a disease if encountered in the future.

implantation   The point during prenatal development at which the developing organism attaches itself to the thick, rich uterine lining.

induction of labor   Various procedures, such as puncturing the amniotic sac or giving hormones to stimulate contractions, that can begin or speed up labor.

information processing   A theoretical approach that emphasizes how the mind manages and organizes information.

insecure ambivalent attachment   A pattern of attachment; children exhibiting this form of attachment show little exploration, are overly upset when separated from a caregiver, not soothed by the caregiver's presence, and alternate between wanting to be comforted and resisting contact.

insecure avoidant attachment   A pattern of attachment; children exhibiting this form of attachment avoid contact with a caregiver, especially when distressed, and show no preference for a caregiver over a stranger.

integrity versus despair   Erikson's final stage, a period when older adults reflect on their lives and search for meaning.

intellectual disability   A type of developmental disability that begins during childhood and is characterized by global delays in cognition.

intelligence   The ability to think, plan and solve problems.

intelligence quotient (IQ)   A general term for a score from an intelligence test.

interdisciplinary   An approach that draws on many different fields of study, ultimately using the theories and methodologies from the various fields to create new theories and methods.

intervention programs   Programs designed to minimize the dangers and consequences of risky behaviors that have already occurred and to prevent future occurrences of these risky behaviors.

intimacy versus isolation   Erikson's sixth stage, it occurs during adulthood and involves finding an intimate, loving relationship.

kangaroo care   A method of newborn care that snuggles the baby against a parent's bare chest to maintain skin-to-skin contact; this keeps the baby warm and allows the baby to hear a heartbeat just as if it were still in the womb.

lanugo   a soft down hair that covers the body of the fetus and helps the vernix stick to the skin.

lateralized   a term used to explain that each hemisphere of the brain has its own functions.

learning disability (LD)   A diagnosis given when there is a difference between a student's academic performance and potential.

leptin   A protein produced by fat cells thought to be the main trigger for puberty.

lesbian   A female sexually attracted to other females.

longitudinal research   A research method that follows the same individuals over a long period of time.

low-birth-weight (LBW)   A baby weighing less than 5½ pounds at birth.

make-believe play   A form of play during which objects are used to stand for something else.

malnutrition   A deficiency in nutrition; the leading cause infant mortality.

maltreatment   Any non-accidental physical or psychological injury; includes physical abuse, sexual abuse, emotional abuse, and neglect.

maturation   Development occurring according to a naturally unfolding sequence.

medicalization of childbirth   Excessive use of medical technologies during childbirth.

menarche A girl's first menstrual period.

menopause A biological change in females that occurs during middle adulthood and marks the end of menstruation and fertility.

mental retardation A term once commonly used to refer to a generalized disability characterized by slower learning and development. In diagnoses, this term has been replaced by intellectual disability.

metabolism The complex chemical reactions that take place inside cells converting calories into energy for the body.

metacognition Thinking about one's own thoughts and thought processes.

middle childhood The period between age 6 and age 12, also called the school years.

middle-age-spread Excessive weight gained during middle adulthood.

midlife crisis A time when an individual faces aging and mortality and wants to make life changes.

Montessori School A school based on the educational philosophy of Maria Montessori, which emphasizes children's work and exploration.

moratorium A time when an individual is in the process of exploring his or her identity but has not yet made a commitment.

mortality when participants leave a study before it is done so the researcher has more participants at the start of the study than at the end.

multidirectional influence The individual influences the environment, and that environment in turn influences the individual.

multiple intelligences Several different types of abilities or talents that enable people to think and to solve problems.

myelin A fatty substance wrapped around the axon to protect it and help messages travel quickly.

naming explosion The time period around 12 to 24 months of age when children learn new words very rapidly.

natural childbirth A birth that occurs when mothers and partners are educated about childbirth and have an active say in the decisions surrounding the child's birth.

naturalistic observation Scientific observations made in the regular or typical environment.

nature One's biological make-up and genetic components.

nature-nurture debate A philosophical debate that questions which is more influential on the individual, the environment or biological make-up.

neglect Guardians not providing for the physical or emotional needs of a child or other dependant.

nervous system   A system comprising the brain, spinal cord, and neural tissue throughout the body.

neural plasticity   The idea that the pattern of connections between neurons can be altered by experiences.

neural tube   The tube-like structure that eventually becomes the spinal cord and brain; during the embryonic period, this is where neurons are formed before traveling to their final destination.

neuron   A cell that is part of the nervous system and is primarily responsible for sending and receiving messages from other neurons; nerve cell found in the brain and spinal cord.

neurotransmitters   Chemicals released by the axon and picked up by the dendrite and enable communication between neurons.

No Child Left Behind (NCLB)   Federal laws that link federal money to scores on standardized tests intended to measure school achievement. The goal of NCLB is to ensure that every child (regardless of income, ethnicity, or background) achieves basic academic success matching or exceeding a previously determined basic level.

norm group   A representative sample of people whose test scores are used as a standard against which future test takers' scores are compared.

norm-referenced tests   Tests that compare the scores of test takers to those of a representative group of individuals previously given the test.

norms   Age-related averages of some measurement of development, obtained from large samples of individuals.

nuclear family   Heterosexual married parents and biological children.

nurture   Environmental experiences one has when interacting with others; how one is raised.

object permanence   Understanding that things continue to exist even when they cannot be sensed.

onlooker play   A type of play that occurs when a child watches and interacts with others, but is not an active part of the play.

operation   Moving things around; a process or a series of steps.

overproduction   When axons and dendrites grow and make more synaptic connections than are needed.

overregulation   Applying grammar rules to "irregular" words that do not conform to typical patterns (e.g., She teached me, I saw the mouses).

ovum   The human egg, or female sex cell, that contains genetic information and a large store of nutrients.

oxytocin   A hormone that triggers uterine contractions.

parallel play A type of play that occurs when children are near each other, pay attention to each other, and are engaged in similar activities, but play independently.

parenting style Beliefs and strategies that guide parents' childrearing behaviors.

peer influence *See* friend's influence.

peer pressure A group encouraging a person to engage in a behavior or change a belief so that it conforms with group behavior or belief.

peers Individuals of the same age and situation.

percentile rank A score given to represent the percentage of people from the norm group who scored at or below that score.

permissive indifferent A parenting style characterized by a lack of involvement, often neglectful.

permissive indulgent A parenting style characterized by warmth, affection, communication, and few rules.

persistent vegetative state A condition in which the brain stem (responsible for vital functions) works, but the cortex (which controls awareness and thought) does not.

personal fable The feeling of uniqueness common to adolescents, which can result in feeling misunderstood or invincible.

pervasive developmental disorder (PDD) A group of disorders that involve delayed development of social and communication skills.

philosophy Field of study that relies on reasoning to discover meaning or truth.

physical abuse Non-accidental injury resulting from behaviors such as hitting, kicking, burning, or shoving.

pituitary gland A small gland at the base of the brain, which secretes hormones that control other glands.

plasticity Flexibility.

post-formal A stage of cognitive development when individuals are pragmatic, expect contradictions, and consider social situations when making decisions.

pragmatism Real-life limitations are included in thoughts.

prenatal development Growth and change to an organism during pregnancy.

preoperational stage Piaget's second stage of cognitive development, which takes place between age 2 and age 7. During this stage, symbolic thought increases, but children are unable to use logical thought.

preterm   A baby born less than 35 weeks after conception.

prevention programs   Programs designed to educate individuals and stop certain behaviors before they appear.

private speech   Speech that occurs when children talk out-loud or whisper to themselves as an aid to solve problems or direct behavior.

proximodistal principle   A principle stipulating that growth occurs from the spine outward, or from near to far.

pruning   The loss of unused synaptic connections.

psychoanalytic theories   A class of personality theories that emphasize internal forces as the main influence on development.

psychology   The scientific study of the human mind, behavior, and emotions.

psychometrics   The field of study that scientifically measures individual differences in psychological traits.

psychosexual stages   Stages of personality development that emphasize a child's sexual drives and the role parents play in permitting or limiting the gratification of those drives.

puberty   The biological changes that mark the beginning of adolescence and lead to adult size and the ability to sexually reproduce.

punishment   The presentation of something negative or the removal of something positive after an unwanted behavior on the premise that this will decrease the likelihood the behavior will recur.

Pygmalion effect   *See* self-fulfilling prophecy.

quasi-retired   Gradually reducing work hours or becoming less involved with work.

reaction time   The length of time it takes to respond to something, reflecting how quickly the brain works.

receptive language   The ability to understand language.

refrigerator mother   A derogatory term once used to describe the mothers of autistic children, stemming from the erroneous belief that the disorder was caused by the mothers' lack of warmth.

reinforcement   Presentation of a reward or the removal of something negative after a desired behavior on the premise that this will increase the likelihood the behavior is repeated.

respiratory distress syndrome (RDS)   A medical condition that occurs when a baby's lungs do not produce enough surfactant to work on their own and the baby stops breathing.

reversibility   Mentally reversing the steps used to solve a problem.

risk taking Engaging in behaviors that are potentially dangerous or deadly.

role overload Something that occurs when adults have difficulty managing the numerous roles they occupy.

Rosenthal effect The influence of a teacher's expectations on a child's learning; *also see* self-fulfilling prophecy.

scaffolding A technique from sociocultural theory for teaching that breaks tasks down into manageable pieces, provides material or hints and tips if needed, offers encouragement, and then gradually removes these supports as the task is mastered.

secular trend A historical trend indicating a change in body size or timing of development.

secure attachment An attachment pattern characterized by infants who can separate from a caregiver, explore the environment, and seek comfort and be consoled by the caregiver when distressed.

self-fulfilling prophecy When others expect an individual to perform a particular way, they will.

sensitive period A broad span of time when it is optimal for something to happen in the environment in order for some ability to emerge.

sensorimotor stage Piaget's stage of development between birth and age 2 when children use their senses and motor skills to understand the world.

separation anxiety Distress a baby signals by crying or protesting when separated from caregiver.

sequential research A research method that combines longitudinal and cross-sectional methods. At the beginning of the study there are a number of different age groups; these are then studied over a period of time.

sexual abuse Any non-consensual sexual contact between two individuals, including touching and non-touching offenses. Because children can never give consent, all adult- child sexual contact is abusive.

sexual orientation The tendency to be consistently attracted to individuals of the same (homosexual), the opposite (heterosexual), or both (bi-sexual) sexes.

singlehood Not living with an intimate partner.

sleeper-effects Consequences that do not appear immediately but surface later.

small for gestational age A baby born smaller than would be expected given the time since conception.

social cognition How people think about the social world, including other people, social situations, social institutions, and the self.

social smile   A smile in response to a face.

sociocultural theory   A theory that states development takes place in the context of interactions between the individual and his or her social and cultural world.

solitary play   A type of play that occurs when a child plays alone and makes no effort to engage others.

sonogram   An image obtained from an ultrasound.

sperm   The males sex cell that carries genetic information to the ovum.

standardized   A procedure or test conducted the same way every time and scored with clear and consistent scoring methods.

standardized test   A measurement that is administered and scored the same way for all test takers, so that there is fairness for all.

standards based education reform   An approach to improving learning that sets standards and then tests students to see if they have met those standards.

stem cells   Undifferentiated cells that can become any type of cell in the body.

Strange Situation   A standardized laboratory procedure that measures the attachment relationship between infant and caregiver.

stranger anxiety   Clinging to a caregiver or showing sadness when a stranger is present.

Sudden Infant Death syndrome (SIDS)   A seemingly healthy infant between 2 and 12 months of age stops breathing while asleep and dies.

surfactant   A chemical produced by a fetus' lungs, which keeps the air sacs in the lungs open.

synapse   The space where the axon of one neuron connects with a dendrite of another neuron.

temperament   Individual differences in emotions, activity, and self-regulation, which are genetically determined but are also influenced by experiences.

teratogens   Any environmental substance that can damage the developing organism during pregnancy.

theory   A set of ideas used to explain some phenomenon.

transgender   Individuals who are labeled one sex at birth but feel they are truly the opposite sex.

trimesters   A popular non-scientific way to divide pregnancy into three equal time periods, each lasting three months

Trisomy-21   *See* Down's syndrome.

trust versus mistrust Erikson's first psychosocial crisis when infants learn trust or learn they can not rely on others.

ultrasound A medical device that uses high-frequency sound waves; the echoes are then transformed into an image called a sonogram.

umbilical cord The cord that connects the prenatal organism to the placenta, delivering nutrients and removing waste.

undifferentiated A characteristic of cells during prenatal development when all cells are exactly the same. Undifferentiated cells are also called stem cells.

unoccupied play A type of play that occurs when there is no interaction, the child is not involved with others who are playing.

vaccine *See* immunization.

vernix A white wax-like substance that coats the fetus and protects its skin from chapping due to exposure to the amniotic fluid.

very low birthweight (VLBW) A body weight at birth of less than 3 pounds 5 ounces.

visual cliff A piece of equipment used to measure depth perception that looks like there is a drop from one side of a table to another.

wisdom Having knowledge and good judgment and the ability to apply these to everyday problems.

youth The life period between adolescence and adulthood, that usually occurs between that ages of 19 and 25. Also called early adulthood or emerging adulthood.

zone of proximal development A concept from sociocultural theory stipulating that there is a range of skills that can be learned with the assistance of a mentor and that learning does not occur if tasks are too far above or below that range.

zygote The newly fertilized cell that results from the union of the egg and sperm.

BIBLIOGRAPHY

Brewster, A., J.P. Nelson, T.R. McCanne, D.R. Lucas, and J.S. Milner. "Gender Differences in Physiological Reactivity to Infant Cries and Smiles in Military Families." *Child Abuse and Neglect* 22, no. 8 (1998): 775–778.

Bronfenbrenner, U. "Toward an Experimental Ecology of Human Development," *American Psychologist, 32* (1977): 513-531.

DeCasper, A.J., and Spence, M.J. "Prenatal maternal speech influences newborns' perceptions of speech sounds." *Annual Progress in Child Psychiatry and Child Development:* (1986): 5-25.

Elkind, D. "Egocentrism in adolescence." *Child Development* 38 no. 4 (1967): 1025-1034.

Erikson, E. *Identity: youth and crisis.* Oxford England: Norton & Co., 1968.

Flavell, J.H. "The Development of Children's Knowledge About the Appearance-reality Distinction." *American Psychologist* 41 (1986): 418–425.

Flavell, J.H., B.H. Everett, K. Croft, and E.R. Flavell. "Young Children's Knowledge About Visual Perception: Further Evidence for the Level 1–Level 2 Distinction." *Developmental Psychology* 17 (1981): 99–103.

Frodi, A.M., and Lamb. M.E. "Sex Differences in Responsiveness to Infants: A Developmental Study of Psychophysiological and Behavioral Responses." *Child Development* 49 (1978): 1182–1188.

Gottman, J. *Why Marriages Succeed or Fail… and How you can make yours last.* New York, NY: Simon & Schuster, 1994.

Hetherington, E.M. and Kelly, J. *For Better or For Worse: Divorce Reconsidered.* New York NY: W.W. Norton & Company, 2003.

Horn, J.L. and Cattell, R.B. "Refinement and test of the theory of fluid and crystallized general intelligences." *Journal of Educational Psychology,* 57 (1966): 253-270.

Hubel, D.H. and Wiesel, T.N. "Receptive fields, binocular interaction and functional architecture in the cat's visual cortex." *Journal of Physiology,* 160 (1962): 106-154.

Jenny, C., T.A. Roesler, and K.L. Poyer. "Are Children at Risk for Sexual Abuse by Homosexuals?" *Pediatrics* 94, no. 1 (1994): 41–44.

Kristensen, P. and Bjerkendal, T. "Explaining the relation between birth order and intelligence." *Science* 22 (2007)1717. DOI: 10.1126 /science.1141493.

Langer, E. and Rodin, J. "The effects of choice and enhanced personal responsibility for the aged: A field experiment in an institutional setting" *Journal of Persoanlity and Social Psychology,* (1976) 191-198.

Larson, R., M. Richards, G. Moneta, G. Holmbeck, and E. Duckett. "Changes in Adolescents' Daily Interactions with Their Families from Ages 10 to 18: Disengagement and Transformation." *Developmental Psychology* 32 (1996): 744–754.

Marcia, J. "Development and validation of ego identity status." *Journal of Personality and Social Psychology* 3 no. 5 (1966): 551-558.

NICHD Early Child Care Research Network. "Early Child Care and Children's Development Prior to School Entry: Results from the NICHD Study of Early Child Care." *American Educational Research Journal* 39 (2002): 133–164.

Parten, M. "Social participation among preschool children." *Journal of Abnirmal and Social Psychology,* 28 (1932): 136-147.

Piaget, J. *Origins of intelligence in the child.* London: Routledge & Kegan Paul, 1936.

Rosenthal, R. and Jacobsen, L. *Pygmalion in the classroom: teacher expectation and pupils' intellectual development.* New York: Holt, Rinehart and Winston, 1968.

Rosenzweig, M.R., Krech, D., Bennett, E.L., Diamond, M.C. Effects of Environmental complexity and training on brain chemistry and anatopmy: a replication and extension." *Journal of Comparative and Physiological Psychology* 55: (1962): 429-437.

Savin-Williams, R.C. *Mom, Dad. I'm gay. How families negotiate coming out.* Washington DC: American Psychological Association, 2001.

Saxe, G.B. "The Mathematics of Child Street Vendors." *Child Development* 59 (1988): 1415–1425.

Schaie, W. *Developmental influences on adult intelligence: The Seattle longitudinal study.* New York, NY: Oxford University Press, 2005.

Sheehy, G. *Passages: Predictable crises of adult life.* New York, NY: Bantam Books, 1976.

Sinnott, J.D. *The Development of Logic in Adulthood: Post-formal Thought and Its Applications.* New York, NY: Plenum Press, 1998.

Smetana, J. and Gaines, C. "Adolescent-parent conflict in middle class African American families" *Child Development,* 70 no. 6 (1999): 1447-1463

Steiner, J.E. Human Facial Expressions in Response to Taste and Smell Stimulation. In. H.W. Reese and L.P. Lipsitt (Eds.), *Advances in Child Development and Behavior, Vol. 13* (pp. 257–296). New York: Academic Press, 1979.

U.S. Department of Health & Human Services, Administration on Children Youth & Families. *Child Maltreatment 2007.* Washington, D.C.: U.S. Government Printing Office, 2009. Retrieved July 21, 2010 from http://www.acf.hhs.gov/programs/cb/pubs/cm07/index.htm.

White, A. "A Global projection of subjective well-being: A challenge to positive psychology?" *Psychtalk, 56* (2007): 17-20.

Zeskind, P.S., J. Sale, L.A. Maio, L. Huntington, and J.R. Weiseman. "Adult Perceptions of Pain and Hunger Cries: A Synchrony of Arousal." *Child Development* 56 (1985): 549–554.

INDEX

Note: Page numbers followed by g indicate glossary entries

R

Rauscher, Frances 42
reaction time 76–77, 143*g*
receptive language 143*g*
refrigerator mother 66, 143*g*
reinforcement 9, 143*g*
research methods 10–13
residential communities, adult 126–127
respiratory distress syndrome 20, 143*g*
retirement 126
Rett's syndrome 66
reversibility 61–62, 78, 143*g*
risk taking 144*g*
    in adolescence 99, 102, 103
Rodin, Judith 127
role overload 124–126, 144*g*
Romanian orphans 40, 42, 81–82, 132*g*
Rosenthal, Robert 106
Rosenthal effect 107, 144*g. See also*
    expectancy effects
Rosenzweig, Mark 40
Rousseau, Jean-Jacques 8

S

safety 60–61
same-sex partners 122
Savin-Williams, Richard 107
Saxe, Geoffrey 78
scaffolding 63, 144*g*
Schaie, Werner 117
schools 84. *See also* education
school years. *See* middle childhood
SECC study (NICHD) 67–68
secular trend 98, 144*g*
secure attachment 48–49, 144*g*
self-fulfilling prophecy 107–109, 144*g*
sensitive period 41–43, 144*g*
sensorimotor stage 45, 144*g*
sensory deprivation/stimulation 40–43
sensory skills 44–45
separation anxiety 46, 144*g*
sequential research 12–13, 144*g*
sex 125
sex hormones 96–97
sexual abuse 89, 144*g*
sexual maturation. *See* puberty
sexual orientation 106–107, 122, 144*g*
Shaw, Gordon 42

Sheehy, Gail 120
siblings 87–88
Simon, Théodore 79
singlehood 124, 144*g*
Sinnott, Jan 101
Skinner, B. F. 9
sleep, in infants 34–35
sleeper-effects 29, 144*g*
small for gestational age 26, 144*g*
Smetana, Judith 105
smoking, in pregnancy 21
social and emotional development
    in adolescence 102–109
    in adulthood 121–128
    in early childhood 70–72
    in infants and toddlers 46–49
    in middle childhood 84–90
social cognition 101–102, 144*g*
social interaction, and learning 59,
    63–64
social relationships
    in adolescence 105–109
    in adulthood 121–123
social smile 145*g*
sociocultural theory (Vygotsky) 59, 63–64,
    69, 145*g*
solitary play 71, 145*g*
sonogram 22–23, 145*g*
South Africa 75
Spain 74–75
speech
    child-directed 65, 133*g*
    private 64, 143*g*
sperm 15, 145*g*
standardized 145*g*
standardized procedure 48
standardized tests 82–84, 145*g*
standards-based education reform 83–84,
    145*g*
Stanford-Binet test 79–80, 82
Steiner, Jacob 44
stem cells 18, 145*g*
stranger anxiety 46, 145*g*
The Strange Situation 48, 49, 82, 145*g*
Sudden Infant Death Syndrome (SIDS) 33,
    35, 36, 145*g*
surfactant 20, 145*g*
Sweden 53–54, 71
synapses 38, 145*g*